GW00733456

# LISTS
# LONDONERS

*Third Edition*

Jeremy Gibson and Heather Creaton

Federation of Family History Societies
in association with the Centre for Metropolitan History

First published 1992 by the
**Federation of Family History Societies.**

Third edition published 1999 by
Federation of Family History Societies (Publications) Ltd.,
2-4 Killer Street, Ramsbottom, Bury, Lancs. BL0 9BZ, England;
in association with the
Centre for Metropolitan History, Institute of Historical Research,
University of London, Senate House, Malet Street, London WC1E 7HU.

First edition, 1992, reprinted 1993.
Second edition, 1997.
Third edition, Copyright © Heather Creaton and Jeremy Gibson, 1999.

ISBN 1 86006 107 9

Typeset from computer discs prepared by the authors
and printed by Parchment (Oxford) Limited.

Cover graphics by Linda Haywood.
Cover illustration of St. Paul's from Ludgate Hill kindly provided by
the Greater London Local History Library and Record Office Picture Library.

### Acknowledgements

Filling in questionnaires is a time-consuming occupation, and one which faces record offices, libraries and individuals with increasing frequency. We are very grateful to all those who completed the Centre's form, thus providing the initial information listed in this guide and generously making it accessible to others. Directly or indirectly much information comes from various 'Gibson Guides', so thanks are due also to the many who helped with those. At stages of its long gestation Sue Lumas and Cliff Webb have commented helpfully on the various drafts and updated details.

In this third edition we add our thanks to the many individuals who took the trouble to reply to our fresh circulation; and to tell us of specific additions and alterations needed, which we are always pleased to receive. Pressure of time and work prevented a circulation of public repositories. We apologise for omission of any recently compiled lists, and will be very pleased to hear of any suitable for future inclusion.

**H.C. and J.S.W.G.**

Federation of Family History Soceties (Publications) Ltd. is a wholly owned subsidiary of
the Federation of Family History Societies, Registered Charity No. 1038721.

# CONTENTS

# Preface

This guide represents the first collaboration between the Centre for Metropolitan History and the Federation of Family History Societies in providing information for all those working on the history of London. We hope it will lead to further useful joint projects. The idea was born at one of the Centre's seminars, when discussion after the paper revealed the existence of several unpublished indexes or biographical listings of people who lived or worked in London at various periods of history. Many of these lists had been generated during work on a book, thesis or article, but had not themselves been incorporated in the final publication. It seemed a pity that the results of so much labour should not be more widely available, so the Centre decided to collect as much information as possible with a view to publishing a guide to these sources. A pleasant feature of this project has been the generosity with which the compilers of the data have offered use of it to others, to save duplication of effort.

The Centre's questionnaire was sent to all members on its mailing list, to the London record offices and local history libraries, and to family history societies. This resulted in the return of over three hundred completed forms.

At a later stage it was felt that to provide information on unpublished indexes and lists without indicating the already published material these were supplementing might seem like 'Hamlet without the prince'. Such publications are myriad, so this is only attempted in certain fields. In those already covered in the 'Gibson Guides' series in which this booklet appears some explanation of the original sources and their arrangement is given. Other information has been augmented from guides previously published by the Society of Genealogists.

For this third edition, all individual contributors and family history societies listed in the second edition were circulated afresh, and a large percentage responded. A few of these have at their request withdrawn their entries. Many have amended them. If no reply was received from an individual, their name, address and entry have been allowed to remain, with the caveat 'No update received.' On this occasion pressure of time and work did not allow a circulation of libraries and record offices. They may now have further lists and indexes of relevance, and we will be pleased to hear of these for future notice.

Since this Guide first appeared, Stuart Raymond has compiled several invaluable bibliographies, *Londoners' Occupations: A Genealogical Guide*, 1994, *London and Middlesex* (2nd edition, two parts): *Essex* (2 parts), and *Kent* (3 parts), 1997-98, all published by the F.F.H.S. These of course deal with printed, published works, so admirably complement this Guide, which relates mainly to unpublished finding aids.

We are under no illusions that the listing is complete, and would be most grateful to hear of any omissions or corrections with a view to keeping the details as up to date as possible.

## The entries

The title of the list or index is given first, followed by a rough estimate of the total number of names covered. The abbreviated name of the compiler or holding institution follows in italics. Their full names and addresses are given on pages 7-10. In the sections on the census and on electoral registers this arrangement is slightly different.

# Addresses and Abbreviations

Please remember to send a stamped and addressed envelope when writing to request information. Details of fees payable can often be found in Gibson and Hampson, *Marriage and Census Indexes for Family Historians*, FFHS (7th edition, 1998). Addresses of family history societies are for information on publications and membership.

**Allen,** Dr D.E., Lesney Cottage, Middle Road, Winchester, Hants. SO22 5EJ.

**Armourers** Hall, 81 Coleman Street, London EC2R 5BJ. 0171-606 1199.

**Ayton,** Mr Clive, P.O. Box 19, West P.D.O., Nottingham NG8 5JE. [Fee payable.]

**Barking** Public Libraries, Valence Reference Library, Becontree Avenue, Dagenham, Essex RM8 3HT. 0181-595 8404.

**Battersea** Library, 265 Lavender Hill, London SW1 1JB. 0181-871 7467.

**Baxter,** Mr J.H., 16 Chandos Parade, Benfleet, Essex SS7 2HT. [Fee payable.]

**Bell,** Dr M., School of English, University of Birmingham, Edgbaston, Birmingham B15 2TT.

**Bexley** Local Studies Centre, Hall Place, Bourne Road, Bexley, Kent DA5 1PQ. 01322 526574 ext. 217/218.

**BL:** British Library, 96 Euston Road, London NW1 2DB.

**Bourne,** Mrs S., 26 Brookside Road, Istead Rise, Northfleet, Kent DA13 9JJ. [Fee payable.]

**Bowers,** Mr R.C., Road End Cottage, Stockland, Honiton, Devon EX14 9LJ.

**Bradley,** Dr H., c/o Institute of Historical Research, Senate House, Malet Street, London WC1E 7HU. [No update received.]

**Bratton,** Dr J.S., Drama Dept., Royal Holloway and Bedford New College, Egham, Surrey TW20 0EX. [No update received.]

**Brent:** Community History Library, 152 Olive Road, London NW2 6UY. 0181-450 5211.

**Bromley** Central Library, High Street, Bromley, Kent BR1 1EX. 0181-460 9955 ext. 261/2

**Broughton,** Mrs T., 43 Pertwee Drive, Great Baddow, Chelmsford, Essex CM2 8DY. [Fee payable.]

**BRS:** British Record Society, Hon. Sec.: P.L. Dickinson, Richmond Herald, College of Arms, Queen Victoria Street, London EC4V 4BT.

**Burns,** Mr Terry, 39 Bolton Lane, Hose, Melton Mowbray, Leics. LE14 4JE.

**Camden** Local Studies and Archives Centre, Holborn Library, 32-38 Theobalds Road, London WC1X 8PA. 0171-413 6342.

**Campop:** Cambridge Group for the History of Population, 27 Trumpington Street, Cambridge CB2 1QA.

**Centre for Kentish Studies,** County Hall, Maidstone ME14 1XQ. 01622 694363.

**Chapman,** Mr Richard, 15 Willerton Lodge, Bridgewater Road, Weybridge, Surrey KT13 0ED

**Chelsea** Local Studies Library, Chelsea Old Town Hall, Kings Road, London SW3 5EE. 0171-352 6056/2004.

**Clark (1),** Mr Geoffrey, 30 Albert Palace Mansions, Lurline Gardens, London SW11 4DG. [No update received.]

**Clark (2),** Dr Gillian, 12 Squirrels Way, Earley, Reading, Berks. RG6 2QT.

**Clifford,** Dr H., Victoria and Albert Museum, London SW7 2RC.

**Clifton,** Dr G., 55 The Ridgway, Sutton, Surrey SM2 5JX.

**CLRO:** Corporation of London Records Office, P.O. Box 270, Guildhall, London EC2P 2EJ. 0171-332 1251

**CMH:** Centre for Metropolitan History, Institute of Historical Research, Senate House, Malet Street, London WC1E 7HU. 0171-636 0272 ext. 40.

**Cook,** Mr S., 20 Cautley Close, Quainton, Aylesbury, Bucks. HP22 4BN.

**Cottrell,** Mr R.J., 19 Belleview Road, Bexleyheath, Kent DA6 8ND. [Fee payable.]

**Creaton,** Miss H.J., c/o **CMH.**

**Croydon** Local Studies Library, Central Library, Katharine Street, Croydon CR9 1ET. 0181-760 5400.

**Ealing** Local History Library, 103 Ealing Broadway Centre, London W5 5JY. 0181-567 3656 ext. 37.

**East of London FHS,** c/o David Filby, 19 Cavendish Gardens, Ilford, Essex IG1 3EA.

**East Surrey FHS,** c/o Mrs R. Turner, 27 Burley Close, London SW16 4QQ.
(Bookstall Manager: Miss Sue Adams, 10 Cobham Close, South Wallington, Surrey SM6 9DS.)

**Enfield** Local History Unit, Southgate Town Hall, Green Lanes, London N13 4XD. 0181-982 7453.

**English Heritage,** London Region, 23 Savile Row, London W1X 1AB. 0171-973 3000.

**Ensing,** Miss R.J., 103 Engadine Street, London SW18 5DU.

**FFHS:** Federation of Family History Societies.

**Finsbury** Library, 245 St. John Street, London EC1V 4NB. 0171-278 7343.

**Fowler,** Mr S., 13 Grovewood, Sandycombe Road, Kew, Richmond, Surrey TW9 3NF.

**Fulham:** see **Hammersmith.**

**Gandy,** Mr M.J., 3 Church Crescent, Whetstone, London N20 0JR. [Fee payable.]

**Genealogists:** Society of Genealogists, 14 Charterhouse Buildings, Goswell Rd, London EC1M 7BA. 0171-251 8799. [A fee is payable for use of the Library by non-members.]

**GLRO:** *see* **LMA.**

**Green (1),** Dr D., Department of Geography, King's College, Strand, London WC2R 2LS. [No update received.]

**Green (2),** Mr E., History Department, Royal Holloway and Bedford New College, Egham, Surrey TW20 0EX. [No update received.].

**Greenwich** Local History Library, Woodlands, 90 Mycenae Road, London SE3 7SE. 0181-858 4631.

**Guildhall** Library, Aldermanbury, London EC2P 2EJ. 0171-332 1863.

**Gunnersbury** Park Museum, Gunnersbury Park, London W3 8LQ. 0181-992 1612.

**Hackney** Archives Department, 43 De Beauvoir Road, London N1 5SQ. 0171-241 2886.

**Hammersmith** and Fulham Archives and Local History Centre, The Lilla Huset, 191 Talgarth Road, London W6 8BJ. 0181-741 5159.

**Hardyman,** Mr B.J.M., 6 Beeforth Close, New Earswick, York YO32 4DF.

**Haringey:** Bruce Castle Museum, Lordship Lane, London N17 8NU. 0181-808 8772.

**Hertfordshire** County Record Office, County Hall, Hertford SG13 8DE. 01992 555105. [Research service fee may be payable for lengthy searches requested by post.]

**Hillingdon FHS,** c/o Mrs G. May, 20 Moreland Drive, Gerrards Cross, Bucks. SL9 8BB.

**Iillingdon** Heritage Service, Central Library, High Street, Uxbridge, Middx. UB8 1HD. 01895 250702.

**Iolborn** Library: *see* **Camden**.

**Iounslow:** Local Studies, Hounslow Library Centre, 20 Treaty Centre, High Street, Hounslow, Middx. TW3 1ES. 0181-570 0622.

**Iunter**, Mrs J., 26 Wood Lane, Cippenham, Slough SL1 9EA.

**Hyde**, Mr R., c/o Guildhall Library.

**IHGS:** Institute of Heraldic and Genealogical Studies, 79-82 Northgate, Canterbury, Kent CT1 1BA. [Fee payable. Parochial maps of London, Middlesex, Surrey, Kent etc. available.]

**Islington** Central Reference Library, 2 Fieldway Crescent, London N5 1PF. 0171-609 3051.

**James**, Mr N.W. & Mrs V.A., 9 College Street, St. Albans, Herts. AL3 4PW.

**Jones**, Mrs D., 95 Oakington Avenue, Wembley, London HA9 8HY. [Fee payable.]

**Kensington** Central Library, Hornton Street, London W8 7RX. 0171-937 2542.

**Kingston** Heritage Service, North Kingston Centre, Richmond Road, Kingston-upon-Thames, Surrey KT2 5PE. 0181-547 6738.

**La Rocca**, Fr. J.J., Xavier University, Cincinatti, Ohio 45207-4444, U.S.A. [No update received.]

**Lambeth** Archives Department, Minet Library, 52 Knatchbull Road, London SE5 9QY. 0171-926 6076.

**Lambeth Palace Library**, London SE1 7JU. 0171-928 6222.

**Lewisham** Local Studies and Archives, Lewisham Library, 199-201 Lewisham High Street, London SE13 6LG. 0181-297 0682.

**Lincoln's** Inn Library, London WC2A 3TN. 0171-242 4371.

**Liu**, Dr T., History Department, University of Delaware, Newark, Del. 19716, U.S.A. [No update received.]

**LMA:** London Metropolitan Archives (formerly GLRO), 40 Northampton Road, London EC1R 0HB. 0171-332 3824.

**London & North Mdx FHS**, Hon. Sec., c/o Mrs S. Lumas, 7 Mount Pleasant Road, New Malden, Surrey KT3 3JZ.

**McGuinness**, Emeritus Professor R., Music Department, Royal Holloway and Bedford New College, Egham, Surrey TW20 0EX.

**Meaden**, Mrs L., Springfield Cottage, Morleys Road, Weald, Sevenoaks, Kent TN14 6QY. [Fee payable.]

**Mercers'** Company, Mercers' Hall, Ironmonger Lane, London EC2. 0171-726 4991.

**Merton** Central Reference Library, Wimbledon Hill Road, London SW19 7NB. 0181-946 1136.

**Mesley**, Dr R.J., 21 Charts Close, Cranleigh, Surrey GU6 8BH. [Fee payable.]

**Metropolitan Police** Museum, c/o Room 317, New Scotland Yard, Broadway, London SW1H 0BG.

**Morris**, Mr D.B., 21 Haddon Court, Shakespeare Road, Harpenden, Herts. AL5 5NB.

**Neller**, Mr D., 8 Elleray Road, Teddington TW11 0HG. [No update received.]

**Newham** Local Studies Library, Stratford Reference Library, Water Lane, London E15 4NJ. 0181-557 8856.

**NW Kent FHS:** North West Kent FHS, c/o Mrs B. Attwaters, 141 Princes Rd, Dartford, Kent DA1 8HJ.

**Nutt**, Mrs J.D.E., 15 Westfield Close, Wickford, Essex SS11 8JR. [Fee payable.]

**Pearce**, Mr K.R., 29 Norton Road, Uxbridge Road, Middx. UB8 2PT.

**Powell**, Mr A.E., 71 Whitestile Road, Brentford, Middx. TW8 9NR. [Fee payable; no update received.]

**PRO**: Public Record Office, Ruskin Avenue, Kew, Richmond, Surrey TW7 4DU. 0181-876 3444.

**Ramsay**, Dr N., Top Flat, 22 Upper Wimpole Street, London W1M 7TA. [No update received.]

**Raymond**, S.A. & M.J., PO Box 35, Exeter EX1 3YZ.

**Rhind**, Mr N., 3 The Lane, London SE3 9SL.

**Selon**: South East London Index - *see* **Shilham**.

**Shilham**, Mr P.R., 6 Beckford Close, Wokingham, Berks. RG41 1HN. [Fee payable.]

**Smith**, Mr S.G., 59 Friar Road, Orpington, Kent BR5 2BW. [Fee payable.]

**Southwark** Local Studies Library, 211 Borough High Street, London SE1 1JA. 0171-403 3507.

**Spencer-Silver**, Mrs P., 26 Muncaster Road, London SW11 6NT.

**Surrey** History Centre, 130 Goldsmith Road, Woking, Surrey GU21 1ND. 01483-594594.

**Survey** of London, 55 Blandford Street, London W1H 3AF.

**Sutton** Central Library, St. Nicholas Way, Sutton, Surrey SM1 1EA. 0181-770 4747.

**Tanner**, Mrs S., 2 Hospital Road, Sevenoaks, Kent TN13 3PH.

**Taylor**, Dr C., 51 Earls Court Square, London SW5 9DG.

**Tower** Hamlets Local History Library & Archives, Bancroft Library, 277 Bancroft Rd, London E1 4DQ. 0181-980 4366, ext. 129.

**Veale**, Dr E.M., c/o Institute of Historical Research, Senate House, Malet Street, London WC1E 7HU. [No update received.]

**Waltham** Forest Vestry House Museum, Vestry Road, London E17 9NH. 0181-509 1917 or 527 5544 ext. 4391.

**Watts**, Mr R., 34 Cherry Orchard, Wotton-under-Edge, Glos. GL12 7HT.

**Webb**, Mr C.R., Cold Arbor, Coldharbour Road, Pyrford, Surrey GU22 8SJ. [Fee payable.]

**West Middlesex FHS**, c/o Mrs M. Burton, 10 West Way, Heston, Middx. TW5 0JF..

**Westminster AC**: Westminster Archives Centre, 10 St. Ann's St., London SW1P 2XR. 0171 798 2180.

**Westminster & Central Mdx FHS**: c/o Miss D.M. Heywood, 46 Churchill Place, Harrow, Middx. HA1 1XY.

**West Surrey FHS**, c/o Mrs R. Cleaver, 17 Lane End Drive, Knaphill, Woking, Surrey GU21 2QQ.

**Whyman**, Dr S.E., 153 Buttonwood Drive, Fairhaven, NJ 07704, USA. [No update received.]

**Winser**, Miss A., 6 Berkeley Row, Lewes, East Sussex BN7 1EU.

**Worms**, Mr L., Ash Rare Books, 153 Fenchurch Street, London EC3M 6BB.

**Wright**, Mr David, 71 Island Wall, Whitstable, Kent CT5 1EL. [Fee payable.]

**Zahadieh**, Dr N., Economic History Department, University of Edinburgh, Edinburgh EH8 9YL. [No update received.]

**Zouch**, Miss J., 132 Larch Crescent, Yeading, Hayes, Middx. [Fee payable; no update received.]

# 1. GENERAL LISTINGS

## 1. Wide Areas

Boyd's Inhabitants of London, 15th-19th centuries. 60,000. *Genealogists* (copy of index only also at *Guildhall*).

General index of names: more comprehensive for records from former Middlesex Record Office. Large. *LMA*.

Middlesex deeds registry, 1709-1919 (annual indexes); 1920-38 (on card). Large. Also Ts calendar for 1709-1716, giving names of both parties to transaction. *LMA* (*Westminster AC* also has microfilm index 1709-1837).

Newspaper notices etc.,The Andrews index to, 1890-1972. Large. *IHGS* (compiled by firm of Chancery agents).

Blue plaque files: Biographical material on people commemorated with blue plaques on buildings associated with them. 2,000. *English Heritage*.

## 2. City of London

City names, miscellaneous, index. 3,800. *CLRO*.

Londoners to 1216. 8,000. *CMH* (compiled by S. Reynolds and G. Keir).

Fraternity of St. Nicholas members, 1448-1522. 7,000. *James*.

Freemen of the City, 1495-1649, 1668-9. 16,000. *CLRO*.

Citizens of London, c.1558-1603:, Aldermen, common councillors, city officers etc.). 1,700. *CMH* (compiled by Professor R.M. Benbow). Copy at *CLRO*.

Civil War London, civic leaders (aldermen, common councilmen, London militia officers, masters and wardens of livery companies etc), 1640-60. 1,500. *Liu*.

City freedom admission papers, 1681-1940. c.300,000. *CLRO*.

Non-freemen journeymen, licences granted to freemen to employ, within the City, 1750-1845. 8,500. *CLRO*.

## City of London continued

Property holders in Poultry and Bucklersbury, and in the Minories (St. Botolph Aldgate and Holy Trinity Minories parishes) before the Great Fire. 2,300. *CMH* (comp. D. Keene and others).

Financial centre of London: resident population: 1693, 1815-16, 1851, 1871. 6,500. *CMH* (comp. J. Lawrence).

Finsbury manor freeholders, 1550-1760. 400. *CLRO*.

Finsbury estate: persons and property, 1711-1848. 800. *CLRO*.

City biographies, 1950s-1970s. Large (from City Press and other sources). Large. *Guildhall*.

## 3. Westminster

Westminster archives name index. 200. *Westminster AC*.

Westminster deeds, 16th-20th centuries. 37,300. *Westminster AC*.

Westminster local collection information, 17th-20th centuries. 13,500. *Westminster AC*.

Social, political and literary landmarks of Bath and Piccadilly; annals of the Haymarket, A.M. Broadley collection of scrapbooks, 1711-1911. 2,400. *Westminster AC*.

Berkeley Square trustees' minute books, 1834-1924. 100. *Westminster AC*.

Paddington and St. Marylebone, personal names, 17th-20th centuries. 6,000. *Westminster AC*.

## 4. Other London Boroughs

**Barking** local collection. 8,000. *Barking*.

Personal names in deeds acquired during compulsory purchase in Barking; and in Dagenham, Becontree Housing Estate. *Barking*.

**Bexley** archives, 1300 to date. 15,000. *Bexley*.

**Brent** local collection. 4,500. *Brent*.

**Bromley** archives: names. Large. *Bromley*.

Bromley residents, 1960 to date, with some coverage from 1858 (from local newspaper articles etc). 7,000. *Bromley*.

**General Listings:** *London Boroughs* contd.

**Croydon** biographical index. 100,000. *Croydon.*

Norwood biographical index. 300. *Croydon.*

**Ealing** local history collection (excludes newspapers). 9,000. *Ealing.*

Ealing local newspapers: the Holt index, 1866-1961 (covers former borough of Ealing). 8,300. *Ealing.*

Ealing local newspaper index, 1961 to date. 10,800. *Ealing.*

**Enfield** local collection. 21,000. *Enfield.*

Enfield enclosure award, 1806. 600. *Enfield.*

**Greenwich** local history library collections. 28,000. *Greenwich.* See also Lewisham.

**Hackney** archives collection. 19,000. *Hackney.*

**Hammersmith and Fulham** archives collection. 65,000. *Hammersmith.*

*West London Observer,* 1856-62. 2,500. *Hammersmith.*

**Hillingdon** local history collection. Large. *Hillingdon.*

Uxbridge residents: the McCabe index, 17th-19th centuries. Large. *Hillingdon.*

Uxbridge residents. 3,000. *Pearce.*

**Hounslow:** local personalities, topography etc. 50,000. *Gunnersbury.*

Rothschild family archives of Gunnersbury Park, relating to Ealing and Hounslow, 1925-1970. *Gunnersbury.*

Feltham Index. Census and parish registers, 11,000, comp. by Peter Watson. *Hounslow.*

Isleworth: list of the copyhold tenants of Syon estate, 1780 and 1656. 300. *Genealogists.*

**Kensington** manuscript collection. 12,200. *Kensington.*

Kensington biographical index. 1,300. *Kensington.*

Kensington notable inhabitants. 800. *Kensington.*

*Kensington News,* obituaries, 1889-1900. 150. *Kensington.*

Chelsea local history collection. 25,000. *Chelsea.*

**Kensington** contd.: Chelsea manuscripts collection. 5,000. *Chelsea.*

**Kingston** corporation deeds. 2,500. *Kingston.*

**Lambeth** archives collection. Large. *Lambeth.*

**Lewisham:** Deptford manuscripts, 1647-1885. 540. *Lewisham.*

Blackheath people, 1680-1940 with addresses in modern form (covers as many residents as possible). Large. *Rhind.*

**Newham:** Clayton's survey of the parish of West Ham, 1821. *Newham.*

*Stratford Express* and *Newham Recorder,* index, 1805-1909. *Newham.*

**Richmond:** Teddington. Par. regs., census, misc. sources from 1550 (31,000). *Neller.*

**Southwark** deeds collection. 10,000. *Southwark.*

**Sutton** residents. *Sutton.*

Carshalton residents. *Sutton.*

**Tower Hamlets** local history collection. 80,000. *Tower.*

Tower Hamlets material in the *Gentleman's Magazine,* 1731-1814. 1,000. *Tower.*

St. Matthew, Bethnal Green: estate governors' qualification book, 1823-30. Residents and landowners. 2,000. *Tower.*

Poplar surnames: index to seven volumes of the parish records, together with a progressive street directory for the period 1819-20, 1826-31. 2,400. *Genealogists.*

**Waltham Forest:** Chingford names to 1900. 10,000. *Waltham.*

Leyton residents, 1575-1880. 40,000. *Waltham.*

Walthamstow and Leyton deeds, including Ruckholt court rolls, 15th to 19th centuries. 8,000. *Waltham.*

Walthamstow names, to 1900. 60,000. *Waltham.*

Walthamstow local newspaper index. 10,000. *Waltham.*

For LBs formerly in Essex (Barking, Havering, Newham, Redbridge, Waltham Forest), see also F.G. Emmison, *Essex Genealogical Indexes,* Friends of Historic Essex (reprinted from the *Genealogists' Magazine,* **21**.2, June 1983).

## 2. LISTS CONCERNING PARTICULAR TYPES OF SOURCE

### A. Parish Registers, Marriage Licences etc.

The Harleian Society and other bodies have published many transcripts and indexes to London parish registers, see E.L.C. Mullins' *Texts and Calendars* (1958, 1983). Guildhall Library's *Handlist of Parish Registers*, pts. 1 and 2 (5th rev. edn. 1984, 1986) covers many Anglican parishes in the City and Greater London and notes published indexes where they exist. Their *Handlist of Nonconformist, Roman Catholic, Jewish and burial ground registers* (1986) also mentions any published transcripts.

See also the *Society of Genealogists' Parish Register Copies* pt.1 (10th edn. 1995).

### 1. Wide areas

### a. Parish records

**Erith and Sidcup Deaneries.** 1565-date. *Bexley.*

### b. Births and baptisms (parish and non-parochial registers)

**Essex** baptisms (parish registers only), 1780-1840. Large. *Nutt.*

**Foundlings.** Mostly from City of London church records (18 parishes). c.3,000. *Watts.*

### c. Marriages (parish and non-parochial registers)

For Marriage Indexes, which generally relate to pre-1837 years, areas now thought of as 'London' will be found not only in Middlesex but also in Essex, Kent and Surrey (Southwark in particular).

*Marriage Indexes*

**Boyd.** There is a specifically 'London and Middlesex' section in the main index, but some places may instead be found in the 'Miscellaneous', section, which includes registers throughout the country. Altogether covers 177 parishes etc, but many for part period only, ending 1754 or 1812, others to 1837; some extracts only, incl. some London Marriage Licences and many Huguenot registers. Approx. 73 per cent of the city and county. Parishes and periods covered are listed in *A list of parishes in Boyd's Marriage Index*, 6th ed., Society of Genealogists, 1994. *Genealogists* and *Guildhall.*

*Marriage Indexes continued*

**Pallot.** Virtually complete coverage of metropolis 1800-1837, some from 1780 or 1790. Both parties. Mostly year only. Phonetic. Widows usually shown. Full guide to London parishes covered, £1, or see *The Phillimore Atlas and Index of Parish Registers. IHGS.*

**Catholic Marriage Index, 1837-1870.** Covers 60 parishes in **London** (north of the Thames) and **Essex**. 1837-1870. List of Central London parishes coverage available. *IHGS.*

**Selon Index** (mainly South East London). 20 parishes, 16 from Phillimore. Both parties to 1812 or 1837. All from copies, but already in Boyd. List available. *Shilham.*

**Middlesex** (only): **1813-1837.** Males only, for those parishes outside the City of London not in Boyd or Pallot (see above). 60 per cent to date but many from BTs only, hence gaps. Year only for small parishes, year and month for large. Alphabetical with cross-refs. *Webb.*

**West Middlesex Marriage Index.** 67,000 entries from most parishes in the West Middlesex area and some others up to 1837. *Chapman.*

**Wembley St. John** 1846-1915. M'fiche. *Westminster & Central Mdx FHS.*

**Essex marriages,** mainly 1754-1851, including outer London area (augments Boyd). Large. *Baxter.*

**Hertfordshire:** The Allen index to Hertfordshire marriages to 1837. Large. *Hertfordshire County Record Office.*

**West Kent** marriages, 1538-1812, including parishes in south east London and many strays from other London parishes. c.160,000. *Smith.*

**Kent** marriages, 1813-37, including south east London parishes. 170,000. *Gandy.*

**Surrey** marriages, to 1837, males only. Large. *Webb.*

## d. Marriage licences, bonds and allegations

There is a complex series of published and other indexes to London marriage licences, bonds and allegations. The following details are based on Gibson's *Bishops' Transcripts and Marriage Licences, Bonds and Allegations: A guide to their location*, 4th edition, F.F.H.S., 1997.

A *Guildhall* leaflet summarises holdings of Marriage Licence records for London and Middlesex both at that Library and elsewhere. The **Diocese of London** included, in addition to the City of London, much of Essex and Middlesex, part of Hertfordshire and four Bucks. parishes.

There are alternative published indexes, 16th and 17th centuries. For the relatively few MLs **1520/1-1597**, issued by the 'Vicar General of the Bishop of London', see the full chronological list, with index of names, in Harleian Society **25** (1887).

For **1597-1648** see first British Record Society **62**, and for **1660-1700**, B.R.S. **66**. These are chronological calendars, giving names of parties only, with indexes. Those asterisked are abstracted fully in Harl. Soc. **25** (1597-1610/1) or **26** (1611- 1648, 1660/1-C19 - but very few after 1661).

These volumes contain many inaccuracies, and there are copies with MS amendments and references to extant related bonds, by B. Lloyd, at Guildhall manuscripts enquiry desk.

From 1700 there are the following indexes or calendars available at *Guildhall* manuscripts searchroom:

**1700-1760**, TS indexes of both parties (17 vols.);

**1760-1826**, MS calendars of names of parties, arranged chronologically (6 vols);

**1827-1964**, MS calendars of names of parties, arranged alphabetically within years, by men's name only (6 vols.).

Amongst the unpublished indexes and calendars held at *Society of Genealogists* for the 18th century are:

**1700-1745**. TS index (14 vols.);

**1700-1780**. Great Card Index. The later years may not be completely covered.

**1761-1762**. TS, by Beric Lloyd.

The original allegations, from 1597, are at *Guildhall*, but the original books of the Vicar General to 1685, calendared in full for the 16th century in Harl. Soc. **25**, are at *LMA*.

Also at *Guildhall* are ML records of the:

**Archdeacon of London** (most of the City Clerkenwell, Islington and Shoreditch in Middx.), 1666-91 (index by name of both parties);

**Dean and Chapter of St. Paul's Cathedral,** allegations 1686-1841, bonds 1670-1823 (TS index to grooms' names only). (Jurisdiction: City: St. Faith, St. Giles Cripplegate, St. Gregory, St. Helen Bishopsgate, and Precinct of Portpool; **Middx.**: Friern Barnet, Chiswick, West Drayton, Precinct of Hoxton (Shoreditch), St. Luke Old Street, St. Pancras, Stoke Newington, Willesden; also three parishes in Herts. and six in Essex);

**Royal Peculiar of St. Katherine by the Tower**, allegations 1686-89, and printed calendar, 1698-99, 1755-1802, alphabetical by first letter, then chronological, in *Home Counties Magazine* **4-6**. Also unpublished bonds and allegations for 1720-24 and 1727-1758.

Marriage Licence records for the **Peculiar Deanery of the Arches** are at *Lambeth Palace Library*. These survive from August 1684 to February 1706/7 only. A full abstract calendar is still in preparation, but the index is now available for public consultation. The parishes in the Peculiar were: All Hallows Bread Street, All Hallows Lombard Street, St. Dionis Backchurch, St. Dunstan-in-the-East, St. John the Evangelist Watling Street, St. Leonard Eastcheap, St. Mary Aldermary, St. Mary Bothaw, St. Mary le Bow, St. Michael Crooked Lane, St. Michael Royal, St. Pancras Soper Lane, St. Vedast Foster Lane.

Harrow with Pinner and Hayes with Norwood were in the **Peculiar Deanery of Croydon**, whose Marriage Licence records are also at *Lambeth Palace Library*. A full abstract calendar for the full period, Aug 1684 - Dec 1818, is still in preparation, but the index is now available for public consultation.

Marriage Licence records for the **Peculiar of the Dean and Chapter of Westminster** are published in (apparently) full, fully abstracted, for the whole period they survive: 1558/9-1646, 1661-1678, 1688-1699, in Harl. Soc. **23** (1886). The places in the Peculiar were the precincts of the Abbey, St. Margaret's Westminster, Paddington, precincts of St. Martin le Grand and parts of the parishes of St. Leonard Foster Lane and St. Anne and St. Agnes; also St. Mary Maldon in Essex.

arriage Licences *continued*

*Westminster AC* has an account book of fees 'or MLs issued by the **Dean and Chapter**, 1772-1804; and an indexed collection of MLs 'rom St. Peter, Eaton Square, 1766-1891. It should be borne in mind that very many marriage licences for Londoners were issued by the Archbishop of Canterbury's **Faculty Office** and **Vicar General**, whose Marriage Licence records are described on pages 7-8 of *Bishop's Transcripts and Marriage Licences.*

**Marriage Licences Index.** St. Martin in the Fields 1765-1837; St. Mary, Putney 1822-1837; All Saints, Wandsworth 1827-1837; St. Luke, Chelsea 1713-1837; Holy Trinity, Chelsea 1832-1837; St. Leonard, Shoreditch 1774-1837; St. Dunstan 1731-1837; St. Paul, Deptford 1779-1833; Christ Church, Spittle-fields 1757-1780; St. John, Hackney 1779-1837; St. Paul, Covent Garden 1734-1837; Kensington, Deptford, Whitechapel etc., 1707-1837. *IHGS.*

**London** marriage licences, 1640. 1,300. *Campop.*

**e. Deaths and burials**

**London and Middlesex**, 1538-1853 (males only), Boyd's index to transcribed burial registers. 250,000. *Genealogists* (copy also at *Guildhall*).

London funeral certificates, 16th-early 18th century. 100. *Genealogists* (compiled by P. Boyd).

Bunhill Fields (nonconformist), 1822-54 [MS 1092A] and MIs 1700-1854 (as of 1869) [index MS 897/8]. *Guildhall.*

London inhabitants identified from the burial entries of their children at nurse in parishes outside the capital, 1540-1750. 4,000. *Clark (2).*

City of London burials, 1813-57. 15,000. *Webb/West Surrey FHS.*

St. Botolph outside Aldgate parishioners, 1583-1584, 1588-90, 1598-1600, 1623-4. 4,869. *CMH* (compiled by D. Keene and others).

1665 burial registers: St. Botolph Aldgate, St. Dunstan-in-the-West, St. James Clerkenwell, St. Magnus, St. Michael Queenhithe, St. Mary Colechurch, St. Mary-le-Bow, St. Saviour Southwark. 11,000. *CMH* (compiled by J. Champion).

Essex burials, 1813-65. Large. *Baxter.*

**2. Indexes to registers for specific parishes or places.**
Note that these only represent a small number almost fortuitously compiled by or held in the locations indicated. Very many other registers have been transcribed, indexed and often published. For their existence and location see the works quoted on page 13.

*Westminster*

**Knightsbridge chapel, Holy Trinity.** Baptisms 1674-94 and marriages 1689-1752. 4,800.

**St. George Hanover Square**, baptisms, 1752-1841.

**St. James Piccadilly**, baptisms, 1700-1, 1723-1735, 1741-4, marriages, 1685-1754 (7,200).

**St. John Smith Square**, baptisms, 1729-1837 (19,500); marriages, 1728-54 (800).

**Camden Town for St. Martin-in-the-Fields,** burials, 1806-56. 17,900.

All at *Westminster AC.*

*Other London boroughs*

**Brent:** Willesden parish registers, 16th century to 1865. *Brent.*

Wembley. St John Wembley par regs 1846-1915, St Mary Harrow-on-the-Hill 1801-46. Also Census 1831-81, Card index. *Jones.*

**Hillingdon:** Providence Chapel registers, 1853-1960s. *Hillingdon.*

Ickenham St Giles burials. *Hillingdon FHS.*

**Islington:** St. James, Clerkenwell, marriages, baptisms and burials, 1560-1753. Large. *Campop.*

**Lewisham:** Deptford, St. Paul, marriage licences, 1776-1835. Large. *Genealogists* (by R. Hovenden).

Deptford, St. Paul, burials 1826-37. 4,600. *Lewisham.*

Lee, St. Margaret's, baptisms 1755-1850 (2,200), marriages 1754-1812, and banns to 1793 (1,500), burials 1755-1850 (3,000). *Lewisham.*

**Kent** parishes in south east London, the Selon index to marriages in: Deptford, 1754-84; Charlton, 1653-1809; Woolwich, 1746-54. Large. *Shilham* (list available).

**Southwark** and other Surrey metropolitan parishes. *Shilham.*

**Tower Hamlets:** St. George-in-the-East, burial dues, 1829-54. 18,000. *Tower.*

Stepney Meeting House burials 1790-1853. M'fiche 2. *East of London FHS.*

## B. Wills and Probate

The following notes are based on the 'London and Middlesex' section and other parts of Gibson's *Probate Jurisdictions: Where to look for wills*, 4th edn, FFHS, 1994 (updated 1997):

Since 1858 probate records for Londoners as all others in England and Wales are at the *Principal Registry of the Family Division, Probate Dept., First Avenue House, 42-49 High Holborn, London WC1V 6NP*, with annual printed indexes.

Before 1858 probate was administered by ecclesiastical courts, the city of London and county of Middlesex being in the diocese of London, Surrey in Winchester and N.W. Kent in Rochester; all in the province of Canterbury.

Londoners more than any were likely to make use of the superior court, the Prerogative Court of Canterbury (PCC) (which operated from Doctors' Commons in London itself). Between 1653 and 1660 the only court available to Londoners, as for the rest of the country, was PCC. The probate records themselves are now at the *Public Record Office, Kew*, but with m'f copies available at the FRC in central London. Indexes to wills from the earliest date (1383) to 1700, and admons. from 1559 to 1660, have been published, mainly by the British Record Society (BRS); an index to wills from 1701 to 1749 is published on m'fiche by the Friends of the PRO; and the period 1750 to 1800 has been published by the Society of Genealogists. Annual MS indexes (alphabetical by initial letter only) are available to wills and admons. for those periods to 1858 not already published. There is a consolidated printed index to wills and admons., 1853-1858. Inventories in PCC only survive in quantity for the period 1661 to the early 18th century, and are at *Kew* only. These are now indexed, and very many are for Londoners. Details of these and other indexes to PCC are in *Probate Jurisdictions*.

For Southwark and other parts of London south of the river and formerly in Surrey, wills proved in PCC and other courts with jurisdiction in the county are included in *Union Index of Surrey Probate Records [to] 1650*, ed. Cliff Webb, BRS **99**, 1990; and for PCC alone, in *Index to Surrey Wills proved in PCC 1650-1700*, West Surrey FHS **9**, 1989. For inventories proved in PCC and other courts, see *Index of Surrey Probate Inventories, 16th - 19th centuries*, compiled by Joan Holman and Marion Herridge, Domestic Buildings Research Group (Surrey), 1986.

The jurisdiction of various courts in London and Middlesex is probably more complicate than anywhere else in the country, and the searcher is advised to examine all major courts, split though they are between several record offices and many indexes. Parishes in the city and county are listed on pages 35-39 with a key to jurisdiction(s) (apart from PCC and the Consistory Court) in which they lay.

*London Metropolitan Archives (LMA)*
*(formerly Greater London Record Office).*

**Consistory Court of London.** The superior court (below PCC), with jurisdiction over the whole city and county except peculiars, so it should always be searched in addition to others listed below. Indexes are in preparation for publication by BRS, 1492-1719, meanwhile manuscript indexes (initial letter only), remain in use: 1492, 1508, 1514-1857.

**Archdeaconry of Middlesex (Middlesex Division).** Jurisdiction over 26 parishes in Middlesex. Wills, 1608-1612, 1662-1701, admons. 1667-1701 (MS initial letter index; full index in preparation by BRS); wills 1702-1736 (card index, and in progress); wills 1737-1794, 1799, admons. 1702-1760 (MS index); inventories 1667-1773 (card index).

**Commissary Court of the Bishop of Winchester in the Archdeaconry of Surrey.** Pubd. to 1650 (left); 1752-1857 (WSFHS 3).

**Archdeaconry Court of Surrey.** Pub. to 1650 (left); 1660-1751, 1752-1857 (WSFHS 1).

*Guildhall Library.*
See *Guide to the Archives*; and *A Guide to Genealogical Sources in Guildhall Library*, 2nd edition.

**Commissary Court of London (London Division).** Jurisdiction over about half the parishes both in the city and in the county. Printed index, wills and admons. 1374-1625 (BRS **82, 86, 97**); 1626-49, 1661-1700, A-G, H-S, T-Z (BRS **102, 108, 111**). Wills and admons. 1571-1629 (modern MS index in short periods); 1629-1857 (MS index, initial letter only).

**Archdeaconry of London.** Jurisdiction over about forty parishes in the city and three populous parishes bordering it; includes St. Botolph Aldgate, to which many mariners, dying abroad, were ascribed as residents (otherwise see PCC). Printed index, wills 1393-1421, 1524-1649, 1661-1700, admons. 1564-1649, 1661-1700 (BRS 89, 98). Wills and admons. 1701-1781 (a few to 1807) (MS index).

**Wills and Probate** *continued*

**Peculiar of the Dean and Chapter of St. Paul's Cathedral.** Jurisdiction over four parishes in the city and all or parts of ten in the county. Wills 1535-1672 (MS index); wills 1672-1837, admons. 1646-1837 (MS initial letter index). New index in preparation for publication by BRS.

**Royal Peculiar of St. Katherine by the Tower.** Wills 1689-1772, 1818, admons. 1688-1793 (TS index, for publication by BRS).

*Corporation of London Records Office (CLRO).*
**Court of Husting.** The court of the corporation of the city of London, with jurisdiction in the city and liberties, to 1688 only. Printed index and abstracts, wills 1258-1688 (*Calendar of Wills ... in the Court of Husting*, R.R. Sharpe, 2 vols., 1888-9).

*Lambeth Palace Library.*
**Deanery of the Arches** (Peculiar of the Archbishop of Canterbury). Jurisdiction in thirteen city parishes (only). Wills, admons. and inventories, 1620-1780, 1832 (BRS **98**).
**Deanery of Croydon** (Peculiar of the Archbishop of Canterbury). Jurisdiction included the Middlesex parishes of Harrow with Pinner and Hayes with Norwood. Wills, admons. and inventories 1614-1841 (MS index, also TS index at *PRO* and *Society of Genealogists*).

*City of Westminster Archives Centre, 10 St. Ann's Street, SW1P 2XR (Westminster AC).*

**Royal Peculiar of the Dean and Chapter of Westminster.** Jurisdiction: precincts of the Abbey, St. Margaret's Westminster, Paddington - from *c*.1700 see under consistory and archdeaconry of Middlesex; precincts of St. Martin le Grand, and parts of the parishes of St. Leonard Foster Lane, and St. Anne and St. Agnes.
Wills and admons. 1504-1700 (printed in *Indexes to the Ancient Testamentary Records of Westminster*, A.M. Burke, 1913); also, as above, and to 1820/30 (very few in later period) (printed by HMSO, 1864, never published; another copy at PRO, but very few other copies are known to exist).

*Centre for Kentish Studies, County Hall, Maidstone ME14 1XQ.*

**Western Kent** parishes now part of the metropolis were in the **Diocese of Rochester** (apart from the Deanery of Shoreham, below). Jurisdiction of **Consistory** and **Archdeaconry Courts** was concurrent. Printed index: wills and admons **1440-1561** *(Kent Arch. Soc. 9)* (Consistory only). Consolidated card index, wills only, to both courts, **1498-1857** (noticeable decline in business from *c*.1750). Calendars to admons fron **1562**.
In western Kent 38 parishes were in the **Peculiar of the Deanery of Shoreham.** Original records are now at *the Lambeth Palace Library*, but the *Centre for Kentish Studies* has all these on microfilm.

*Other indexes:*

**Essex:** Index of males from R. Hollingworth Browne's calendar of Essex wills, 1665-1851. From various courts: Consistory of London, Commissary of London for Essex and Herts., Archdeaconries of Essex, Colchester and Middlesex. Large. *Genealogists* (by J.L. Rayment).

Essex wills beneficiaries, 1675-1858: persons named in wills in Essex R.O. whose names differ from testator. Large. *Broughton.*

**London Probate Index.** London and Middlesex wills and admons. All courts except PCC. 1. 1820-1858 complete. 2. 1750-1800 complete. 3. 1801-1819 in progress. *Wright.*

**London testators** 1800, 1830, 1850. Wills. PCC, Commissary Court of London, Consistory Court of London. *Green (1).*

Wills proved in ecclesiastical courts up to 1670 for:
All Hallows Honey Lane, St. Benet Sherehog, St. Botolph Aldgate, St. Christopher-le-Stocks, St. Martin Pomary, St. Mary le Bow, St. Mary Colechurch, St. Mary Woolchurch, St. Mildred Poultry, St. Pancras and St. Stephen Walbrook. Large. *CMH.*

**Westminster:** Ancient testamentary records of Westminster. Large. *Genealogists.*

Westminster probate inventories (Middlesex archdeaconry courts), mainly 17th century Westminster parishes. Large. *LMA.*

## C. Monumental Inscriptions

The Society of Genealogists has published a useful listing of *Monumental inscriptions in the library of the Society*. Part 1, ed. L. Collins (1984), covers southern England, dealing with published as well as unpublished indexes.

### 1. Wide areas

**Essex:** parishes now in metropolitan area: Chingford, West Ham, Leyton, Leytonstone. *Genealogists.*

**Kent:** areas now in London: Crayford, Deptford (Old Meeting House and Church Street Chapel), Footscray, Greenwich St. Alphege, Lee, Lewisham, St. Mary Cray, Sidcup. Varied. *Genealogists.*

**North West Kent.** St. Mary Bexley, Holy Trinity Bromley, All Souls + Union Baptist Crocker-hill, All SS + Baptist Footscray; St Margaret Lee, All SS Orpington. M'fiche. *NW Kent FHS.*

**London and Middlesex:** Heraldry and MIs in churches. *IHGS.*

**Middlesex:** Monumental inscriptions of Acton, Brentford and Isleworth, New Brentford, Brompton, Bunhill Fields, St. Luke King's Road, St. Jude Sloane Court, St. Nicholas Chiswick, Christ Church Westminster, St. James Clerkenwell, Enfield, Feltham, Holy Trinity East Finchley, Friern Barnet, Fulham, Hackney, Hammersmith, Hanwell, Harefield, Harrow, Highgate Chapel, Highgate, Horn-sey, Ickenham, Islington, Kensington, Kingsbury, Limehouse St. Anne, Paddington, St. George Bloomsbury, St. John's Wood, St. Marylebone, St. Pancras, Savoy chapel, Southgate, Stoke Newington, Sunbury, Teddington, Tottenham, Uxbridge, Westminster cemetery, Whetstone, Whitechapel, Whitfield's tabernacle, Willesden. *Genealogists* (more details in the Society's booklet).

**West Middlesex:** Bedfont, Harmondsworth, Isleworth, Laleham, Littleton and Shepperton. m'fiche. *West Middlesex FHS.*

Teddington Cemetery Index. 6,000. *Neller.*

All SS Harrow Weald, Christchurch Roxeth; St Martin Ruislip, St Mary Perivale, St Mary Harrow-on-the-Hill, St Andrew's Old Church Kingsbury, St Mary Northolt, Paines Lane Cemetery Pinner, St Lawrence Little Stanmore (index), St John Wembley (index). M'fiche. *Westminster & Central Mdx FHS.*

*Wide areas continued*

**Surrey:** 112 Surrey churchyards, pre-1866. Large. *Webb.*

Surrey war memorials. 40,000. *Mesley.*

Surrey areas now in London: Barnes, Battersea, Bermondsey St. James, Brixton, Camberwell, Coulsdon, Croydon, Dulwich, Merton, Morden, Richmond, Southwark, Streatham, Sutton, Tooting, Wandsworth. *Genealogists.*

### 2. City of London

M.Is. in City of London churchyards and burial grounds: All Hallows Staining, Holy Trinity Minories, St. Gregory by St. Paul, St. Nicholas Cole Abbey. *Genealogists.*

Bunhill Fields (nonconformist). See page 15.

### 3. Westminster

St. James, Hampstead Road, 1789-1853. 600.
St. John's Wood burial ground, 1825-55. 1,000.
St. Marylebone parish church, chapel and churchyard, 1644-1965. 1,000.
Paddington Street burial ground, St. Marylebone, 1733-1857. 1,000. *Westminster AC.*

### 4. Other London boroughs

**Barnet:** East Barnet churchyard and Totteridge dissenters' chapel (formerly Hertfordshire). *Genealogists.*

**Bexley:** Bexley, Erith, Crayford, Footscray and Sidcup. *Bexley.*

**Hammersmith & Fulham:** Fulham All SS. Church and churchyard (copied 1887). Hammersmith, Chiswick and other church-yards (by W. Mussared). Hammersmith, St. Paul's churchyard, copied 1882 just before the demolition of the old church. *Hammersmith.*

**Hillingdon.** Harefield St Mary, West Drayton St Martin, Northwood Holy Trinity, Cowley St Lawrence. *Hillingdon FHS.*

**Lewisham:** St. Bartholomew's, Sydenham, churchyard, 19th century. 150.
St. Margaret, Lee, old churchyard, 17th-20th centuries. 400.
St. Margaret, Lee, new churchyard, 19th-20th centuries. 283. *Lewisham.*

**Tower Hamlets:** Whitechapel burial ground, graves in, 1777-81 (Society of Friends). *Guildhall* (index to Ms. 22,364).

## D. The Census

### Census Indexes

### 1801-41

There are no official enumerators' nominal returns for the censuses of 1801, 1811, 1821 and 1831. However a number of unofficial lists made by enumerators do survive, and these are listed in detail in *Local Census Listings 1522-1930*, Jeremy Gibson and Mervyn Medlycott (F.F.H.S., 3rd edn., 1997). The 1841 census was the first to list names, but has less information than the 1851 and subsequent censuses. Consequently relatively few have been transcribed and/or indexed. Pre-1851 reported are as follows:

### 1801.
*Middx.:* St James Westminster, Marlborough Street ward. 500. *Genealogists.*

### 1811.
*Middx.:* Hackney St. John. Published. *East of London FHS. Parish Returns series* **1** (1988). New Brentford (1810). Published. *West Middx FHS jnl.* **2** (2) (Spring 1981). *Surrey:* Southwark St. Saviour. *Selon/ Southwark.* Croydon, Mitcham. *Genealogists.*

### 1821.
*Middx:* Hackney St. John. Published, Parish Returns Series **2** (1997). *East of London FHS.* Poplar All Saints. Published, Parish Returns Series **3** (1997). *East of London FHS.* *Surrey:* Southwark Christchurch (West Div.). *Selon/Southwark.* *Kent:* Beckenham, Bromley. *Genealogists.*

### 1831.
*Middx.:* Hackney St. John. Index in prep. *Hackney.* Poplar All Saints (partial). Published, Parish Returns Series **4** (1998). *East of London FHS.* *Surrey:* Southwark St. Saviour, Christchurch, St. Mary Newington. *Selon/Southwark.*

### 1841.
*Middx.:* Edmonton and Enfield. In preparation. *Enfield.* Stoke Newington. In preparation. *East of London FHS.* Hillingdon. *Hillingdon.* Willesden, Kingsbury, Wembley. *Brent.* *Surrey:* Southwark Christchurch; Bermondsey Workhouse. *Selon/Southwark.* Merton and Morden. *Merton.* *Essex:* East and West Ham. *Newham.* *Kent:* Greenwich (present LB). 28,000; Plumstead, Eltham, Kidbrooke, and St. Nicholas, Deptford. *Greenwich.* Erith, Keston, East and West Wickham. *Genealogists.*

There are street indexes to all London RDs for 1841 at the PRO.

| | |
|---|---|
| **1** Kensington | **19** London City |
| **2** Chelsea | **20** Shoreditch |
| **3** St George Hanover Square | **21** Bethnal Green |
| **4** Westminster | **22** Whitechapel |
| **5** St Martin in the Fields | **23** St George in the East |
| **6** St James Westminster | **24** Stepney |
| **7** Marylebone | **25** Poplar |
| **8** Hampstead | **26** St Saviour Southwark |
| **9** Pancras | **27** St Olave Southwark |
| **10** Islington | **28** Bermondsey |
| **11** Hackney | **29** St George Southwark |
| **12** St Giles | **30** Newington |
| **13** Strand | **31** Lambeth |
| **14** Holborn | **32** Wandsworth |
| **15** Clerkenwell | **33** Camberwell |
| **16** St Luke | **34** Rotherhithe |
| **17** East London | **35** Greenwich |
| **18** West London | **36** Lewisham |

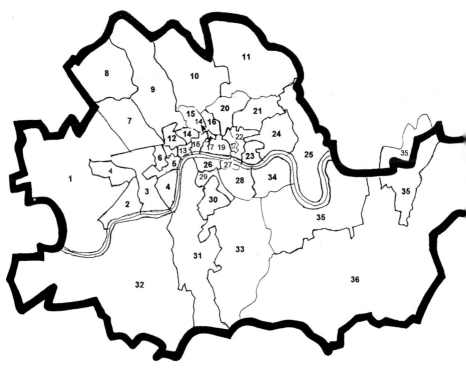

## The Census: 1851.

Most of the 1851 census for the London area has now been indexed thanks to the work of various family history societies. As the census relates to specific registration districts (RDs) and sub-districts, it seems best to list those in the metropolitan area in the numerical order shown in *Making Use of the Census*, by Susan Lumas (PRO Publications, 1997), Appendix 5, pages 75-76 (and see map opposite) and order of PRO Piece Number, as shown in the *1851 Census Index Survey* (FFHS, 1989); with availability of indexes (microfiche unless shown otherwise).

*West Districts of London in Middlesex:*

| 1: | 1466-71 | Kensington | *West Mdx FHS* |
|---|---|---|---|
| 2: | 1472-74 | Chelsea | *West Mdx FHS* |
| 3: | 1475-78 | St. George Hanover Square | *Westminster & Central Mdx FHS* |
| 4: | 1479-80 | Westminster | *Westminster & Central Mdx FHS* |
| 5: | 1481-82 | St. Martin in the Fields | *Westminster & Central Mdx FHS* |
| 6: | 1483-85 | St. James Westminster | *Westminster & Central Mdx FHS* |

*North Districts of London in Middlesex:*

| 7: | 1486-91 | Marylebone | *London & North Mdx FHS* |
|---|---|---|---|
| 8: | 1492 | Hampstead | *London & North Mdx FHS* |
| 9: | 1493-98 | Pancras | *London & North Mdx FHS* |
| 10: | 1499-1502 | Islington | *London & North Mdx FHS* |
| 11: | 1503-06 | Hackney | *East of London FHS – in preparation.* |

*Central Districts of London in Middlesex:*

| 12: | 1507-09 | St. Giles | *London & North Mdx FHS* |
|---|---|---|---|
| 13: | 1510-11 | Strand | *Westminster & Central Mdx FHS* |
| | 1512 | Strand St. Clement Danes | *Westminster & Central Mdx FHS* |
| 14: | 1513-15 | Holborn | *London & North Mdx FHS* |
| 15: | 1516-19 | Clerkenwell | *London & North Mdx FHS* |
| 16: | 1520-23 | St. Luke | *London & North Mdx FHS* |
| 17: | 1524-25 | East London (City without Walls) | *London & North Mdx FHS* |
| 18: | 1526-27 | West London (City without Walls) | *London & North Mdx FHS* |
| 19: | 1528-32 | London City | *London & North Mdx FHS* |

*East Districts of London in Middlesex:*

| 20: | 1533-38 | Shoreditch | *East of London FHS* (book and fiche) |
|---|---|---|---|
| 21: | 1539-42 | Bethnal Green | *East of London FHS* (book and fiche) |
| 22: | 1543-46 | Whitechapel | *East of London FHS* (book only) |
| 23: | 1547-49 | St. George in the East | *East of London FHS* (book and fiche) |
| 24: | 1550-54 | Stepney (incl. Mile End Old Town) | *East of London FHS* (Webb) (fiche only) |
| 25: | 1555-56 | Poplar | *East of London FHS* (book only) |

*South-West Districts then in Surrey (Selon indexes unpublished):*

| 26: | 1557-58 | Southwark Christchurch & St. Saviour | *West Surrey FHS* (and *Selon*, full index) |
|---|---|---|---|
| 27: | 1559 | Southwark St. Olave (SS Thomas, Olave, John Horsleydown) | |
| | | | *West Surrey FHS* (and *Selon/Southwark*) |
| 28: | 1560-62 | Bermondsey | *Selon/Southwark* |
| 29: | 1563-65 | Southwark St. George | *Selon/Southwark* |
| 30: | 1566-68 | Newington | *Selon/Southwark* |
| 31: | 1569-75 | Lambeth | *East Surrey FHS* (and *Selon/Lambeth*) |
| 32: | 1576-79 | Wandsworth | *East Surrey FHS* (and *Selon/Lambeth*) |
| 33: | 1580-82 | Camberwell | *West Surrey FHS* (and *Selon/Southwark*) |
| 34: | 1583 | Rotherhithe | *Selon/Southwark* |

**The Census: 1851** *continued*

*South-East Districts then in Kent:*

| | | |
|---|---|---|
| 35: 1584-85 | Greenwich: Deptford | *NW Kent FHS* (published) |
| 1586-87 | Greenwich: East & West | *NW Kent FHS* (for publication 1999) |
| 1588-89 | Greenwich: Woolwich | *NW Kent FHS* (published) |
| 36: 1590-91 | Lewisham | *NW Kent FHS* (published) |

*Extra Metropolitan (Middlesex):*

| | | |
|---|---|---|
| 47: 1604 | Kingston (Hampton, Teddington) | *West Mdx FHS* |
| 132: 1696 | Staines | *West Mdx FHS* |
| 133: 1697 | Uxbridge | *West Mdx FHS* |
| 134: 1698-99 | Brentford | *West Mdx FHS* |
| 135: 1700 | Hendon | *London & North Mdx FHS* |
| 136: 1701 | Barnet | *London & North Mdx FHS* |
| 137: 1702-04 | Edmonton | *London & North Mdx FHS* |

*Unpublished indexes in local libraries (all also included in some form in above published indexes):*
Enfield and Edmonton. Large. *Enfield.*
Hillingdon (incl. Uxbridge). Large. *Hillingdon.*
Northolt. Large. *Ealing.*
Tottenham and Hornsey, heads of households and independent persons (not dependent wives and children). *Haringey.*

*Essex:*

| | | |
|---|---|---|
| 194: 1768-69 | West Ham (incl. East Ham) | Not yet available. |
| 197: 1772 | Romford | *East of London FHS* (book only). |

*Kent:*

| | | |
|---|---|---|
| 49: 1606 | Bromley | *NW Kent FHS* |
| 50: 1607 | Dartford | *NW Kent FHS* |

Kent-born people in London and Home Counties (except Kent). Large. Unpubd. *Gandy.*

*Surrey:*

| | | |
|---|---|---|
| 46: 1601-02 | Croydon | *East Surrey FHS* |
| 47: 1603-04 | Kingston (incl. Wimbledon) | *East Surrey FHS* |
| 48: 1605 | Richmond | *Fowler* (Richmond LHS) |

*Unpublished indexes:*
Merton and Morden. Large. *Merton* (see also *East Surrey FHS*).
Sutton. *Sutton* (see also *Webb*).

*Other 1851 census indexes:*
London and other prisons: 9,000. Unpubd. *Bourne.*
Kent Strays. Kent-born strays in other counties, including London and Middlesex, Surrey. *Gandy.*
Street indexes to all London RDs; also for Brentford, Croydon, Edmonton, Hendon, Kingston, West Ham. *PRO.*

## 861-91

Indexes to the 1861 census are few. For 871 Mr Clive Ayton is undertaking an ambitious project, see below. The 1881 census, nationwide, has been indexed in a mammoth project by the Mormons. This covers all of London as well as elsewhere.

**1861.**
*Middlesex:* Northolt. *Ealing.*
Hillingdon. Large. *Hillingdon.*
Pancras District 9 (RG9/94-124): Grays Inn Lane, Regents Park, Tottenham Court, Kentish/Camden/Somers Town. District 8 (91-93): Hampstead. *M'fiche.* Burns (copies at *Genealogists, Camden, Guildhall, FRC*).
Willesden, Kingsbury, Wembley. *Brent.*
Willesden (RG9/785, surname, folio, by Robert Hyatt). *Westminster & Central Mdx FHS.*
*Surrey:* Southwark, Christ Church, St. Saviour, St. Thomas. Large. *West Surrey FHS; Genealogists; Southwark; PRO.*
*Kent:* West Wickham. Varied. *Genealogists.*
*Essex:* Barking Town. Alphabetical list of all persons. *Barking.*
East Ham. West Ham (part). Large. *Newham.*
East Ham & Little Ilford (RG9/1058). Published (1997). *East of London FHS* (book only).
Romford R.D. (RG10 1068, pt. 1069, 1072). Published. *East of London FHS* (book only).

Street indexes to all London RDs; also for Brentford, Croydon, Edmonton, Hendon, Kingston, West Ham. *PRO.*

**1871.**
**London Surname Index.** RG10 1-794.
This gigantic project is being undertaken by Clive *Ayton*. Six indexes have been published, each covering five census pieces:
RG10 199-203: Pancras, Regents Park pt 1.
RG10 461-467: Haggerstone West, Shoreditch.
RG10 481-485 Green, Bethnal Green part 1.
RG10 486-490. Green, Bethnal Green part 2.
RG10 580-584. Poplar part 1.
RG10 633-636. St James, Bermondsey pt 1.

130 pieces have been indexed (all RG10): 1-11, 19 (parts of Paddington); 117-19, 124, 136-139, 143-147 (parts of Westminster); 148-154 (part of Marylebone); 199-217, 231 (parts of Pancras); 289-301 (parts of Islington); 342 (part of St. Giles); 421, 434-436 (parts of City of London); 437-440, 461-468 (parts of Shoreditch);

## 1871 continued

**London Surname Index** continued
474-475, 479-490 (parts of Bethnal Green), 580-85 (part of Poplar); 633-641 (part of Bermondsey); 642-643 (part of Rotherhithe); 647-652, 659 (part of Lambeth); 708-11 (part of Wandsworth); 721 (Dulwich); 722-24 (part of Camberwell); 733 (part of Peckham).
*Surrey:* Southwark, Christ Church and St. Saviour's, St Olave, St Thomas, St John Horsleydown, St George the Martyr. *Shilham.*
*Middlesex:* Northolt. *Ealing.*
Enfield and Edmonton. *Enfield.*
Hillingdon. *Hillingdon.*
Bethnal Green [RG10/481-90 only]. *Tower.*
*Kent:* West Wickham. *Genealogists.*

Street indexes to all London RDs; also for Brentford, Croydon, Edmonton, Hendon, Kingston, West Ham. *PRO.*

**1881.**
The 1881 Census has been indexed nationwide and is on m'fiche by county.
*Middlesex:* All Middlesex. *Tower.*
Edmonton and Enfield. *Enfield.*
Hillingdon. *Hillingdon.*
*Kent:* Bexleyheath, Christchurch; Sidcup St. John and Footscray All SS. *Meaden.*
*Essex:* Walthamstow and Leyton. 50,000. *Waltham.*

Street indexes to all London RDs; also for Barnet, Brentford, Bromley, Croydon, Dartford, Edmonton, Hendon, Kingston, Richmond, Romford, West Ham. *PRO.*

**1891.**
Street indexes to all London RDs; also for Barnet, Brentford, Bromley, Croydon, Dartford, Edmonton, Hendon, Kingston, Richmond, Romford, West Ham. *PRO.*

Bethnal Green East [RG12/267-8]. *East of London FHS* (2 books).

Edmonton and Enfield. *Enfield.*

Hampton [RG12/616-8]. *West Middlesex FHS.*

Spitalfields (heads of households only). *Tower.*

Southwark (as for 1871). *Shilham.*

*Indexes based on census returns:*

*Middlesex:* Feltham. All census returns and parish registers). *Hounslow.*

Teddington. Includes census. 31,000. *Neller.*

Wembley. Census 1831-81 – see page 15.

## E. Other Central Government Records

The Public Record Office has many lists and indexes including material on Londoners. For details of their indexes, see *Tracing your ancestors in the Public Record Office* (5th edn. 1999, by Amanda Bevan). Philip Riden's *Record sources for local history* (1987), though it specifically excludes London, nevertheless is an essential source for P.R.O. research. Two books by Stella Colwell, *Family Roots: Discovering the Past in the Public Record Office* (1991) and *Dictionary of Genealogical Sources in the Public Record Office* (1992), particularly the latter, offer much guidance to the finding aids and use of our national archives, for Londoners probably more than elsewhere.

The House of Lords Record Office has some lists of London residents affected by local Acts of Parliament, particularly railway acts.

Court of Requests (debt) bonds and promissory notes, 1613-59. 1,000. *CLRO.*

Returns of divided houses in the City of London, 1637 (includes some areas outside City). Large. *Guildhall* (comp. by T.C. Dale).

Citizens of London 1641-3, from the state papers. 3,150. *Guildhall* (comp. by T.C. Dale).

Recusants indicted, convicted or on the recusant rolls for London and Middlesex, 1603-38. 2,000. *La Rocca.*

## F. Local Administration and Courts

### 1. The City of London

City deeds (miscellaneous, including deeds of Royal Contract estates). 9,300. *CLRO.*

Extents for debt [C131] 1316-1650, for London and Southwark. 2,000 (compiled by M. Catlin). *CMH.*

Court of Common Pleas [CP40], parties to debt cases Michaelmas 1384, 1403, 1424 for London and ten counties. 15,000 (compiled by J. Galloway & M. Murphy). *CMH.*

Corporation of London Journals, 1416-63 (the proceedings of the Court of Aldermen and Court of Common Council). 6,000. *CLRO* (compiled by Dr C. Barron).

Property to 1596: name index to property references in Repertories of Court of Aldermen, Journals of Common Council and unpublished Letter Books. 2,300. *CLRO.*

## Local Administration: City of London *contd.*

Freemen of the city and their sureties in the Recognizance Rolls, 1437-97. 3,600. *CLRO.*

Bridge House deeds (property belonging to Bridge House estates), 12th to mid-18th centuries (most pre-1600). 4,800. *CLRO.*

Bridge House accounts, 1381-1405. 2,800. *CLRO.*

Bridge House rentals, 1404-21, 1460-1509. 9,400. *CLRO.*

City Lands grant books, 1589-1633, and of members of City Lands committee and surveyors of the Chamber's lands, 1589-1652. 4,650. *CLRO.*

City Lands journals, lessees, 1698-1742. 2,000. *CLRO.*

Comptrollers' City Lands deeds: lessees and parties on leases and deeds of title from late 17th century. 7,100. *CLRO.*

Viewers' reports, 1659-1704. 1,600. *CLRO.*

Husting Rolls deeds, 1252-1717. 30,000. *CLRO.*

Sheriffs' Court roll, calendar, 1318, 1320. 1,700. *CLRO.*

Escheat rolls, calendar, 1340-77, 1388-9. 5,800. *CLRO.*

Possessory assizes: novel disseisin, mort d'ancestor and fresh force, calendar, 1340-1591. 3,200. *CLRO.*

Mayor's Court: original bills, Edward III to Richard III; index to parties, temp. Henry VI; index to plaintiffs etc. 1565-c.1725; index to interrogatories, 1628, 1641-1710. 8,000. *CLRO.*

Court of Orphans' Common Sergeants' books, 1586-1614, 1662-1742 (also acts as index to Orphans' inventories). 17,500. *CLRO.*

Fire Court, plaintiffs, 1666-73. 1,100. *CLRO.*

Debtors imprisoned in Fleet, Newgate, Ludgate, Poultry Compter, Wood Street (late Giltspur Street) Compter, 1755-1820, and Borough Compter, 1761-76. 6,000. *CLRO.*

Sessions of the Peace and Gaol Delivery (latter to 1834 only) for the City, 1714-1834, 1855-1927. 134,000. *CLRO.*

Coroners' inquests, London and Southwark, 1788-1837; London, 1838-1921; Southwark, 1838-1921. 47,285. *CLRO.*

# Local Adminstration *continued*

## 2. Westminster

Paddington vestry minutes, 1837-49, 1861-87. Large. *Westminster AC.*

St. Anne Soho, vestry minutes, 1695-1742. 1,600. *Westminster AC.*

St. George Hanover Square, Paving committee minutes, 1771-78, 1782-1831. 6,200. *Westminster AC.*

St. Margaret Westminster, Bastardy depositions, 1711-52. 6,000. *Westminster AC.*

St. Marylebone vestry minutes, 1732-1900. Large. *Westminster AC.*

## 3. Other London boroughs

Tottenham manor, court rolls of, 1318-1582. *Haringey.*

Hillingdon. Extracts of Session Records 1549-1702 from Middlesex County Records, *Hillingdon FHS.*

Earls Court manor court rolls, 1554-1785. 2,800. *Kensington.*

Stratford Langthorne ward court rolls, 1736-1802. *Newham.*

West Ham manor court rolls, 1808-11. *Newham.*

Tower Hamlets Board of Works and Paving Commissions, 1804-80: petitions. 2,500. *Tower.*

Wandsworth: Battersea and Wandsworth manor 1225; Allfarthing and Doune manors c.1360-1540; Wandsworth rectory 1367-1540. Dunsford manor courts, 1559-1751. Names appearing in court rolls. 2,000. *Ensing.*

Wandsworth churchwardens' accounts 1545-1573. *Selon/Lambeth.*

## G. Rates

## 1. The City of London

All Hallows the Great rate lists: for 7th December 1599; for clerks' wages, 1634, and for distressed Protestants in Ireland, 1642. 720. *Genealogists* (compiled by R. Ireland).

St. Martin Orgar rate lists, 1574, 1626 and 1631. 300. *Genealogists* (transcribed by R. Ireland).

## 2. City of Westminster

Voters and ratepayers 1749-1820. From pollbooks (all extant up to 1820, 87,000) and rate books (1784, 1818 in particular). 144,000 on Westminster Historical Database. *Green (2).*

## 3. Other London boroughs

Edmonton rate books, 1764-1850, and valuation lists, 1878, 1884, 1892, 1905. *Enfield.*

Hillingdon Borough Valuation Books, 1910. Index for publication 1999. *Hillingdon FHS.*

St. Mary Magdalen, Bermondsey, poor rate assessment, 1712, and ratepayers, 1699. Large. Selon index. *Shilham.*
See also Poor relief (Southwark).

Bethnal Green ratebook 1850-51. 1,000. *Tower.*

Bow poor rate, 1851. 750. *Tower.*

Bromley St. Leonard church rate, 1861. 750. *Tower.*

Poplar church rate, 1851. 1,500. *Tower.*

Shadwell poor rate, 1725. 1,000. *Tower.*

Wapping church rate, 1875. 350. *Tower.*

Old Artillery Ground drainage rate, 1861. 200. *Tower*

Wapping watch rate, 1800. 400. *Tower.*

Whitechapel watch rate, 1800, 1805. 1,000. *Tower* (compiled by S. Curtis).

All above indexes (except Bethnal Green) at *Tower* available on m'fiche from *East of London FHS.*

## H. Taxes

Records of taxation containing names fall into two main groups. From medieval times to the restoration of Charles II, Subsidies, granted periodically by Parliament, were the main taxation. The lists engendered, temp. Richard II and then from c.1520 on, in general only taxing the wealthiest of the community, are in PRO Class E179.

This class together with SP28 also includes the Collection in Aid of Distressed Protestants in Ireland, 1642, useful for comparison with and supplementing the Protestation Returns of the same year (see section L, page 28). For the City there are lists for 71 parishes (70 per cent) (no Protestation Returns survive). For Middlesex there are 37 parishes, including Chelsea, Ealing, St. Giles in the Fields, St. Marylebone, Westminster St. Margaret, and the upper hamlet of Whitechapel, all missing from the Protestation Returns. Details of all these are given in Gibson and Dell's *The Protestation Returns 1641-42 and other contemporary listings*, FFHS, 1995.

From 1661 on E179 has other useful tax lists, as listed in Gibson's *The Hearth Tax, other later Stuart tax lists and the Association Oath Rolls*, FFHS, 2nd edn., 1996. Little if any transcription, indexing or publication has been undertaken for the City, or for metropolitan Middlesex.

Records of other post-1660 taxes, though national in concept, survive in local repositories, including some magnificent City series, listed in *London Rate Assessments and Inhabitants' Lists in Guildhall Library and the Corporation of London Records Office*, 2nd edn., 1968, and *Guide to the Records at Guildhall*, 1951 (for *CLRO*). Of these, the 1695 'Marriage Tax', is published.

From the 1690s on, after abolition of the Hearth Tax, the Land Tax was the main source of revenue. Records for the City, at *Guildhall*, in 522 volumes, for 1692-94 and 1703-1949, surpass any elsewhere in the country (which mostly only survive from c.1780 to 1832). Land tax assessments for some Middlesex parishes close to the City are also at *Guildhall*, but most for Middlesex, 1767, and 1780-1832, are at *LMA*.

## 1. Wide areas.

**1693-4.** Metropolitan London, 4s. in £ tax. 65,000 (compiled by J. Barnes & C. Spence). *CLRO, CMH.*

## 2. The City of London

**1538.** City of London householders. Large. *Genealogists* (compiled by P. Boyd).

**1662, 1664, 1666.** Hearth Tax returns for: St. Botolph Aldgate, St. Dunstan-in-the-West, St. James Clerkenwell, St. Magnus, St. Michael Queenhithe, St. Mary Colechurch, St. Mary le Bow, St. Saviour, Southwark. 1,500. *CMH* (comp. by J. Champion).

**1663.** Hearth Tax return for Farringdon Ward. Ts. *Genealogists.*

**1692.** Poll Tax. Individual householders, lodgers and others listed incl. information on their assessment for rent and stocks in the 1693 4s. aid (City of London). 25,000 (compiled by J. Alexander). *CLRO, CMH.*

**1695.** Inhabitants of London, within and without the walls. From Marriage Tax assessments. Index to area within the walls superseded by that published in London Record Society, vol. 2 (1966). Large. *Guildhall, CLRO.*

## 3. Westminster

**1625-45.** Westminster inhabitants in the reign of Charles I, from the subsidy rolls, 1625-29, 1640-45. 1,880. *Genealogists.*

## 4. Other London boroughs

**1662-4.** Greenwich. Hearth Tax. 6,000. *Greenwich.*

**1664-74.** Isleworth hundred. Hearth Tax assessments and returns. 960. *Genealogists.*

The Hearth tax has been published for Harrow (1674), Acton (1664-74), Staines (1664), Ealing, Greenford, Hanwell, Northolt, and Perivale (1664-73), also the Poll Tax for Uxbridge 1693/4, see *Hearth Tax...* as above.

**1742-80,** Mile End Old Town residents, from Land Tax, cross-linked to IGI, Livery Company, Insurance, manorial, tithes, Middlesex Deeds Registry, East India Company and licensed victuallers' records. 4,000. *Morris.*

1750. Edmonton. Land Tax assessment. *Enfield.*

1801. St. George in the East. Land Tax assessments. 1,200. m'fiche. *East of London FHS.*

## Tithes

█aling tithe award. 1840. 650. *Ealing.*

█oolwich and Plumstead tithe tenants (1840s). 5,000. *Greenwich.*

## . Poor Relief

See C. Webb, *The Parochial Poor Law records █f Middlesex* (Weybridge, 1986); C. Webb, *█ondon, Middlesex and Surrey Workhouse █ecords: A Guide to their nature and location,* *█est Surrey FHS Research Aid* **31** (1992); █. Gibson, C. Rogers and C. Webb, *Poor Law █nion Records: I. South East England and East █nglia,* FFHS (2nd edn., 1997).

### █. Wide areas

█est Middlesex settlements, covering New Brentford, Chelsea, Ealing, Feltham, Friern Barnet, Fulham, Hammersmith, Hanwell, Shepperton, Staines, Stanwell, Uxbridge. 12,000+. *Zouch.*

█Surrey poor law records. 9,000. *Webb.*

### 2. Westminster

█St. Clement Danes' examination books, 1739-1836. *Westminster AC.*

### 3. Other London boroughs

St. Mary Newington. Indemnity bonds, 1628-1756. Large. Settlement examinations 1783-1801, 1806-21, 1825-46. Workhouse register 1772-84. *Shilham.*

Isleworth poor law and settlement examinations, 1772-1801, 1813-30. Large. *Powell.*

Lambeth, St. Mary: Settlement examinations 1805-07. *Shilham.*

Lambeth Workhouse Report Book. 1816-20. *Shilham.*

Lambeth, Workhouse, Selon index. Admissions' register 1823-33. *Shilham/Lambeth.*

Richmond, people receiving indoor and outdoor relief, 1850-51. 600. *Fowler.*

Richmond Poor Law Union orphans and families emigrating to the colonies, 1834-1930. *Fowler.*

## Poor Relief *continued*

Southwark, St. George the Martyr, Selon index; militia 1807; poor rate 1790; rate deficiencies 1765-66; settlements 1698-1831; workhouse register of parish poor children 1789-1807; register of parish poor 1833; register of illegitimate children 1794-1807. Large. *Shilham.*

Southwark, St. Saviour, Selon index. Settlement examinations 1794-97; recipients of parish relief, 1823-24. *Shilham.*

Southwark, St. Olave, Selon index. Workhouse reports, 1757-83, 1795-1801. *Shilham.*

St. Mary Lambeth: Westminster New Lying-in Hospital, 1805-07. *Shilham.*

St Mary Newington. Recipients of poor relief, 1834-35. *Shilham.*

Tower Hamlets removal orders and examinations, 1703-1865 (persons named in various poor law records). 3,500. *Tower.*

Stratford Bow, St. Mary (1739-62 and 1828-1843), and the liberty of Old Artillery Ground (1792-1836) pauper examination books. Large. *Genealogists* (compiled by I.R. Harrison).

Old Artillery Ground examinations, 1792-1826. *Tower.*

Bromley St. Leonard's poor law examinations, 1778-91. 800. *Tower.*

See also 'Public Health', page 34.

## K. Loans

Chamberlain's records of lenders to royal loans, 1660-70. 1,500. *CLRO.*

St. Clement Eastcheap: list of signatories to loan, 1641, and of feoffees, trustees etc., 1641. 100. *Genealogists* (transcribed by R. Ireland).

### L. Oath Rolls

The best known oath roll is the Protestation of 1641-42, taken by most males over the age of sixteen. See J. Gibson and A. Dell, *The Protestation Returns 1641-42 and other contemporary listings*, FFHS, 1995.

**Middlesex:** The Protestation oath rolls for Middlesex, 1641-2 are published (transcribed by A.J.C. Guimaraens, supplements to the *British* Archivist, 1913-20; republished on microfiche by *North Middlesex FHS*, 1987). Parishes or places covered are: St. Sepulchre; St. Leonard Shoreditch, Clerkenwell; Finchley; Friern Barnet; Hampstead; Hornsey; Islington; Stoke Newington; Willesden; Stepney; St. Leonard Bromley; Limehouse; Poplar and Blackwall; Ratcliff; Stratford Bow; Spitalfields; Bethnal Green; Mile End; Highgate; Edmonton; Enfield; Hadley and South Mimms. Ts index to above. *Guildhall.*

**Surrey:** Published in *The Surrey Protestation Returns 1641/2*, ed. by Hector Carter, Surrey Archaeological Collections **59** (1962), 35-68 and 97-104.

The Association Oath Rolls, 1696, compiled after an attempted assassination of William III, were mandatory on all office holders, but in some parts of the country a great many others took the opportunity to record their loyalty to the Crown and Protestant succession. The original lists, often of actual signatures, are in the PRO [C213], and precise references are given in Gibson's *The Hearth Tax .. and the Association Oath Rolls* (FFHS, 2nd edn., 1996).

**City of London:** PRO lists for the Lord Mayor, Aldermen and Common Councilmen; various City institutions; Guild companies; and the Tower of London.
Typeset (but probably never published) transcripts for the City Livery Companies (32 Companies, Apothecaries to Fruiterers only). *CLRO* and *Genealogists.*

**Middlesex:** PRO lists for County; Militia officers; commissioners of tax; Kensington; Westminster; St. Martin le Grand.

**Surrey:** lists for whole county (incl. Southwark) published on microfiche in *Association Oath Rolls for Surrey, 1695*, tr. Cliff Webb, West Surrey FHS, mf series **3**, 1990.

**Essex and Kent:** see County lists in PRO.

### M. Voters

***Poll Books, 1705-1872.***
Until the reform of 1832 the franchise voting for the two members representing ea county ('knights of the shire') was restricted 40s. freeholders (of whom there were ve many); the qualifications for borough including the City of London, varied greatl and that for Westminster was particularly wid as testified in the famous 1749 election of Jo Wilkes. The secret ballot was not introduce until 1872, and commercial publishers found viable to print poll books showing how ea individual voted. The various published po books for the City and its environs are listed i some detail in J. Sims (ed.), *A Handlist of Britis Parliamentary Poll Books* (1984). A mor concise listing of published and unpublishe poll books is given in Gibson and Rogers, *Po Books 1696-1872*, FFHS, 3rd edn, 1994.

#### 1. The City of London
See W.A. Speck and W.A. Gray, *London Po Books*, London Record Society **17** (1981). There are poll books for 1710-13, 1717-24, 1727, 1734, 1768, 1771-73, 1781, 1784, 1792, 1796 and 1837 (see Gibson, *Poll Books).*
1768 published. *Raymond.*
Index: City of London poll book, 1722. Large. *Guildhall.*
For poll books for wards within the City or for non-parliamentary elections, see Gibson, *Poll Books.*

#### 2. Westminster
There are poll books for 1749 (two elections), 1774, 1780, 1784, 1788, 1790, 1796, 1802, 1806, 1818-20, 1837 and 1841.
1749 published m'fiche. *Genealogists.*
1774, 1818, 1841 published. *Raymond.*
Index: 12,500. *Westminster AC.*
Also: 1798, 1802, St. Margaret and St. John, Westminster; 1832, Paddington, MS poll book. *Westminster AC.*

See also Westminster Historical Database 1749-1820, page 25.

#### 3. London University.
Poll book, 1880. *BL.*

#### 4. County of Middlesex
There are poll books for 1705, 1713-15, 1750, 1768-69, 1772, 1784, and 1802. Also, Tower Division only, for 1806 and 1820 (see Gibson, *Poll Books).*

**lectoral registers, 1832-1915.**
Consequent on the Reform of 1832, annual
gisters of electors were printed. Despite the
uantity initially produced, for the 19th and
arly 20th centuries surprisingly few survive.
The following lists are in three periods, **1832**
 **1885** (when there was a major change in
onstituency boundaries, though there had
een some changes in 1867); **1885 to 1915.**
here were no registers compiled in 1916-17.
1 **1918** there was a further boundary revision
'hich remained in force until **1948**. No attempt
as been made to identify subsequent
onstituencies and local holdings. From 1947
and for most constituencies also for 1937-8) a
omplete set of UK electoral registers is held
y the British Library and these are catalogued
1 Richard H.A. Cheffins, *Parliamentary*
*Constituencies and their Registers since 1832*
The British Library, 1998).
The arrangement is by constituency. From
832 to 1885 there were, in the metropolis, in
ddition to the cities of London and
Westminster, three Middlesex boroughs (rising
o five in 1867), plus Lambeth and Southwark
1 Surrey, and Greenwich in Kent. The
emainder of Middlesex formed one county
division; Surrey was in two (three from 1867)
divisions.
The boundary revision of 1885, followed by
the creation of the County of London in 1890,
eft most of metropolitan London in boroughs.
From 1890 on (1885 for Middlesex) the *LMA*
has complete sets of electoral registers for the
administrative area of the county of London
and the remainder of Middlesex.
Information on holdings is based on Gibson
and Rogers, *Electoral Registers since 1832*
(FFHS, 2nd edn, 1990), with the important
addition of the *BL* collection, based
*Parliamentary Constituencies...*, above.
Locally held post-1918 registers are also
listed in *Electoral Registers*, and individual
constituencies (and subsequent boundary
changes) are given in Youngs, *Local*
*Administrative Units 1* (Royal Historical
Society, 1979, 1980). Identification of pre-1948
constituencies is based on this invaluable
work. The *BL* has 1918-31 runs for Finsbury,
Hammersmith, City of London, Paddington and
Stepney; also for Brentford and Chiswick,
Enfield, Harrow, Hendon, Spelthorne,
Twickenham, Uxbridge and Wood Green, in
Middlesex. Thereafter the *BL* collection,
countrywide, is virtually complete for 1937-38
and from 1947 on.

Indexes:
*Guildhall:* London voters, 1853. 20,400.
*Tower:* Tower Hamlets, 1834-5. 600.

The City of London formed a single borough
constituency until 1948:
**City of London** (1832-1948).
*Guildhall:* 1832-1915, 1918-39, 1945-date
 (except 1954). Index 1853 (20,400).
*CLRO:* 1840, 1872-1915 (missing 1897,
 1903), 1918-39, 1945-date.
*LMA:* 1833-4, 1837, 1855.
*BL:* 1832, 1840, 1848, 1859-1915 (missing
 1871-1872), 1918-31, 1937-38, 1947-date.
*Genealogists:* 1836 (part).

---

| **1832-1885** |
|---|

**County of Middlesex.**
*Guildhall:* 1837, 1860-1863, 1870-1884.
*BL:* 1862, 1865-74, 1878-79.
*LMA:* 1832-43 (overseas returns of electors
 1847-1867), 1883-85.
*Hammersmith:* 1837/8; 1843-46, 1880.
*Genealogists:* 1840. *PRO:* 1874.
Parts only.
*Enfield:* Edmonton 1833; Edmonton and
 Enfield 1862, 1865-6, 1868, 1870, 1872-4,
 1878-9; Enfield 1832, 1837.
*Hackney:* Hackney: Hackney 1834, 1841;
 Shoreditch 1843, 1845; Stoke Newington
 1861.
*Camden:* St. Andrew Holborn within 1843,
 1853, 1855.
*Tower:* 1834 (Tower Hamlets indexed, 600),
 also Ratcliff 1838-9, 1841-54; Whitechapel
 1875.

**Middlesex Boroughs.**
**Camden.** *Camden:* 1964-on.
 *Camden:* Hampstead 1899-1963. *BL:* 1897-8.
 *Camden:* St. Pancras 1886-97, 1899,
 1900/1-1963. *BL:* 1905-15.
**Chelsea** (from 1867). *Chelsea:* 1881-1885.
 *Hammersmith:* 1881-85.
**Finsbury.** *LMA:* 1832, 1865, 1873-89
 *BL:* 1857-8.
 *Camden:* Holborn (only) 1878 (also part 1837).
 *Finsbury:* Clerkenwell 1842; Finsbury 1873-
 1885; 1901-1915.
 *Islington:* St. Mary Islington only 1860.
**Hackney** (from 1867). *Hackney:* 1879; Hackney
 only 1871; Stoke Newington only 1883.
**Marylebone** (1832-85 incl. St. Pancras).
 *Camden:* 1866-71, 1873-7, 1879-85.
 *Westminster AC:* 1844-8, 1850-1, 1854-5;
 Paddington (only) 1867.

**Electoral Registers 1832-1885** *continued*
**Middlesex Boroughs** *continued*

**Tower Hamlets** (1832-85).
LMA: 1833-65 (missing 1855), 1873-89.
Tower: (part constituency: Bethnal Green 1865; Poplar 1833, 1835, 1849).
BL: (part constituency: St. George's 1839-40).
(See also under Middlesex.)
**Westminster** (1832-1918). LMA: 1839-40, 1844, 1850-1, 1858, 1864-5, 1873-89.
Westminster AC: 1857-1859, 1862, 1864-5, 1883, 1906-14.

**County of Surrey.**
Surrey History Centre, Woking, has a very good collection, from 1832 on, for all constituencies in the county. A detailed guide has been prepared and is available for consultation at the S.H.C.

**Eastern Division** (1832-67):
Guildhall: 1859, 1861-4, 1866.
BL: 1864.
**East Division** (1867-85):
BL: 1869-70, 1872.
PRO: 1872.
**Mid Division** (1867-85): BL: 1869-70, 1872.
PRO: 1872.
**Western Division** (1832-85): Croydon: 1851;
BL: 1860, 1863-4, 1866, 1869-70, 1872;
PRO: 1872.

**Metropolitan Surrey Boroughs.**
**Lambeth** (1832-85): Lambeth.1832-1915 (also Streatham: 1832, 1841-2, 1850).
**Southwark** (1832-85):
Southwark: Bermondsey 1848; Camberwell 1832-3, 1835 (part); Newington 1833-85; Rotherhithe 1865; Southwark 1839, 1862.

**Metropolitan Kent Borough.**
**Greenwich** (1832-1885):
Greenwich: 1837, 1845, 1868, 1870-1, 1875.
BL: 1874-85.

| **1885-1918** (but effectively to 1915 only). |
| --- |

**County of Middlesex,** all divisions (Brentford, Ealing, Enfield, Harrow, Hornsey, Tottenham, Uxbridge).
LMA: 1885-1918.
BL: 1891-1915 (Brentford from 1889).

**Divisions:**
**Brentford.** Ealing: Norwood North only 1913.
**Ealing.** Ealing: 1890-1914 (missing 1898).
**Enfield.** Enfield: 1890-1914 (missing 1898).

**Electoral Registers 1885-1918** *continued*

**Middlesex Boroughs:**
LMA: all boroughs 1885-89; all administrative County of London, 1890-1918).
**Bethnal Green (North-East, South-West).**
Tower: 1901-15;
BL: 1897-98, 1900.
**Chelsea.**
Chelsea: 1885, 1887, 1889, 1891-1915.
BL: 1897-1900.
**Finsbury (Central, East, Holborn).**
Finsbury: All divisions 1901-15;
Holborn (only) 1893-1915.
BL: 1891-1915.
**Fulham:**
Hammersmith: 1885, 1887-91, 1895-1915.
BL: 1897-1901.
**Hackney (Central, North, South).**
Hackney: 1889 (Central only), 1901.
BL: 1897-1901.
**Hammersmith.**
Hammersmith: 1886, 1889, 1890-1915.
BL: 1897-1915.
**Hampstead:** Camden: 1899-1915.
BL: 1897-98.
**Islington (East, North, South, West).**
Islington: 1885-1915.
BL: 1897-1901.
**Kensington (North, South):**
Kensington: 1890-1905, 1908-1915.
BL: 1897-1902.
**Marylebone (East, West).**
Westminster AC: 1905; 1912 (West only).
**Paddington (North, South).**
Westminster AC: 1902-15.
BL: 1897-1901, 1904-6, 1908-1910, 1914-5.
**St. George Hanover Square.**
BL: 1885/6, 1892-1900, 1902-4.
**St. Pancras (East, North, South, West).**
Camden: 1886-97, 1899-1915.
BL:1905-15.
**Shoreditch (Haggerston, Hoxton).**
See LMA left.
**Strand.** BL: 1885-1905.
**Stoke Newington.** Hackney: 1893-1916.
**Tower Hamlets (Bow and Bromley, Limehouse, Mile End, Poplar, St. George, Stepney, Whitechapel).**
Tower: 1901-15; Bow 1894-1895; Bow, Bromley, Spitalfields 1898.
BL: 1897-1915.
**Westminster:**
Westminster AC: 1906-14.
BL: 1892-1900, 1902-4.

**Electoral Registers 1885-1918** *continued*

**Metropolitan Surrey Boroughs** (all within administrative County of London): *LMA:* 1890-1918.

**Battersea and Clapham (Battersea, Clapham).**
*Battersea:* 1885-1915.
*BL:* 1897.

**Camberwell (Dulwich, North, Peckham).**
*Southwark:* 1913-5; 1897 (Dulwich only); 1898 (North only).
*BL:* 1897-1901.

**Lambeth (Brixton, Kennington, North, Norwood).**
*Lambeth:* 1885-1915.
*BL:* 1897-1901 (Kennington and North only).

**Newington (Walworth, West).**
*Southwark:* 1885-1900. Walworth only, 1905.
*BL:* 1906-15.

**Southwark (Bermondsey, Rotherhithe, West).**
*Southwark.* 1886-1901, 1904-15.
*BL:* Bermondsey 1887-1915; Rotherhithe 1885-1915; West 1894-1915.

**Wandsworth.**
*Battersea:* 1898-1900, 1907-14.

**Metropolitan Kent Boroughs.**
*LMA:* all within administrative county of London, 1890-1918.

**Deptford.**
*BL:* 1886, 1888-91, 1897.

**Greenwich.**
*Greenwich:* 1892-1915 (gaps).
*BL:* 1874-85, 1901.

**Lewisham.**
*BL:* 1886-89, 1897, 1899 (also county electors 1889).

**Woolwich.**
*Greenwich:* 1900-14.

## 3. THEMATIC LISTINGS

See also S.A. Raymond's bibliographies *Occupational Sources for Genealogists*, 2nd edition, 1996 (FFHS); and *Londoners' Occupations: A Genealogical Guide*, 1994 (FFHS).

### A. Political Parties

West London Labour Index. An index of Labour, Communist and other progressive parties and groups' members active in London Boroughs of Ealing, Hammersmith and Fulham, Hillingdon, Hounslow and Richmond. 4,000. *Neller.*

### B. Local Government Officers and Officials

#### 1. Wide areas

London local government members and officials, 1850-1965 (mainly Metropolitan Board of Works and London County Council). 1,000. *Clifton.*

Middlesex county officials (J.P.s etc.), 16th-20th centuries. Small. *LMA.*

#### 2. The City of London

Lord Mayors, 12th-20th centuries. c.670. *Guildhall, CLRO.*

Sheriffs, temp. Edward the Confessor to date. 1,225. *CLRO.*

Aldermen in London with their wards, and Common Councilmen, 1285 (on flyleaf of Kearsley's London Register, 1787 [A.3.1. no.25]). 67 (also published in *Calendar of Letter Book A*, R.R. Sharpe, London, 1899, pp. 209-10). *Guildhall.*

Mayor's household, officers of, before 1600. 300. *CLRO* (compiled by B. Masters).

Common Councilmen, prior to 1880 and 1880 to date. 6,300. *CLRO.*

Aldermen of the City, 1913 to date. 510. *CLRO.*

#### 3. Westminster

St. Marylebone Borough Council Civil Defence staff, 1939-45. 2,500. *Westminster AC.*

## C. Commerce, Trade and Industry

For trade directories, see The Directories of London, 1677-1977, by P.J. Atkins (1990); and British Directories: a bibliography and guide to directories published in England and Wales (1850-1950)..., by G. Shaw and A. Tipper (1988). Many of these directories are available in a microform collection: London Directories from the Guildhall Library, 1677-1899 (1975).

In the 20th century telephone directories are an obvious source.

Life insurance policy holders and their beneficiaries, 1698-1770. 16,000. *Clark (1)*.

Sun and Royal Exchange fire insurance policy registers, 1775-87. Large. *Guildhall*.

Grinsell's Charity apprenticeship indentures, St. Margaret, Westminster, 1676-1889. 650. *Westminster AC*.

Kent apprentices and masters, 1799-1837 (taken from P.R.O. apprenticeship books, City registers etc). 9,000. *Bourne*.

Merchants and trades, 1660-1720 (contacts of John Verney, Levant merchant). 10,000. *Whyman*.

Colonial trade in 1686 (covers merchants, captains). 200,000. *Zahedieh*.

Tradesmen's cards, 18th-early 19th centuries. 350. *Westminster AC*.

Goldsmiths and silversmiths of Southwark, 1200-1800. *Shilham*.

Garrard ledgers, Parker and Wakelin, 1764-76 (goldsmiths, clients, workmen). 10,000. *Clifford*.

Silver spoonmakers, 1750-1830. 150. *Tanner*.

Storr Paul apprentices, 1790-1820. *Tanner*.

Glassmakers and allied trades, 1600-1900. Many thousands for U.K. *Hardyman*.

Gunmakers. List of tradespeople from a wide variety of sources for the period up to the 1881 census. 7,500+ surnames. *Cook*.

Scientific instrument makers (including barometer makers, globe makers, nautical instrument makers, opticians and scale makers), 1550-1850. 10,000. *Clifton*.

Book trade (women in), 1540-1730. 200. Published in *Leipzier Jahrbuch zur Buchgeschichte* no. **6**, 1996, pp.13-45. *Bell*.

Engravers of maps and prints, 16th - mid-19th centuries. 4,000. *Worms*.

Gillow (furniture makers') waste book, 1729-1744. 450. *Westminster AC*.

Gillow estimate sketch books, 1784-1825. 3,300. *Westminster AC*.

Piano manufacturers, 1835-1930. Over 2,000. *Winser*.

Medieval skinners and men connected with the fur trade. 500. *Veale*.

Textile workers in River Cray area (Bexley and Bromley), 1841-81. 1,500. *Bexley*.

Building firm George Myers & Sons, of Lambeth, 1842-75, business associates and contacts of (includes architects). See *Pugin's Builder: The Life and Work of George Myers*. Hull U.P. 1993. *Spencer-Silver*.

Match girls' strike register, 1888 (Bryant & May employees). 600. *Tower*.

Combmakers, 1660-1920s. 2,000+. *Bowers*.

Combmakers (many in London). *Watts*.

George Inn, Southwark, licensees, leasors and owners of, 1558 to date. 50. *Hunter*.

Funerals undertaken by W. Garstin & Sons, of 49 Wigmore Street, 1834-1952. 28,000. *Westminster AC*.

Funerals undertaken by W. Tookey & Sons of 51 Marylebone High Street, 1888-1931. 5,000. *Westminster AC*.

## Livery Companies

Leaflet available from *Guildhall* Library: ~~~ources for tracing apprenticeship and ~~~embership in City Livery Companies and ~~~lated organisations at Guildhall Library'.

~~~st of freemen of the City companies resident in London and Westminster, [1537], really 1538. Extracted from vol. 2 of T. Allen's *History of London, Westminster and Southwark* (1837). 2,500. *Guildhall*.

Members of the City companies in 1641 as set forth in the poll tax return, compiled by T.C. Dale. 7,500. *Guildhall*.

Liverymen of London in 1700 from the sworn list printed in 1701, together with the names of those in poll book of 1710 but not in 1700 list, compiled by T.C. Dale. 12,400. *Guildhall*.

Armourers and Brasiers' Company of London, freemen and apprentices in the, 1535-1700, compiled by C. Cooper. Large. *Armourers*.

Carpenters' Company records, persons in the, 16th-19th centuries. Large. *Guildhall*.

Coachmakers' and Harnessmakers' Companies, apprentices of the, 1677-1800. 3,500. *Genealogists* (compiled by G. Elland).

Cutlers' Company, apprentices of the, 1687-90, 1712-19. 550. *Genealogists* (compiled by G. Fothergill).

Dissolved companies and bankrupticies, early 19th century. London and Middlesex. *IHGS*.

Drapers' Company, apprentices of the, 1615-1750. Large. *Genealogists* (comp. by P. Boyd).

Gold and Silver Wyre Drawers' Company, List of masters, clerks and beadles of the, 1693-1891. Large. *Genealogists*.

Gunmakers' Company, prior to 1881. List of apprentices and freedoms of the Worshipful Company. *Cook* - see also under section C.

Mercers' Company, list of members of the, from 1347. 6,000. *Mercers'*.

Mercers' Company members before 1527. 2,500. *Mercers'*.

Mercers' Company apprentices, 1619-1890 2,500. *Mercers'*.

Merchant Taylors' Company, apprentices, company freedoms and masters of the, 1538-1818. 2,200. *Genealogists*.

Paviours' Company, apprentices of the, 1565-1783. 550. *Genealogists* (compiled by G. Fothergill).

Pewterers, yeomanry or freemen of the Worshipful Company of 1687-1909. 2,400. *Genealogists* (compiled by H.H. Cotterell).

Scriveners (comp. B. Brooks et al.). *IHGS*.

Stationers' Company apprentices and freemen, 1562-1640. 2,000. *Genealogists* (Boyd).

Watermen's Company, apprentices of the, 1692-1908. Large. Pub'd on fiche. *Cottrell*.

The *Society of Genealogists* is publishing a series of 'London Apprentices' taken from Livery Company records, compiled by Cliff Webb – forty companies to date:

1. Brewers 1685-1899.
2. Tylers and Bricklayers 1612-44, 1668-1800.
3. Bowyers 1680-1806; Fletchers 1739-54, 1767-1808; Longbow-stringmakers 1604-1668, 1709, 1714-17.
4. Glovers 1675-79, 1735-48, 1766-84.
5. Glass-sellers 1664-1812; Woolmen 1665-1828.
6. Broderers 1679-1713, 1763-1800; Combmakers 1744-50; Fanmakers 1775-1805; Framework-knitters 1727-30; Fruiterers 1750-1815; Gardeners 1764-1850; Horners 1731-1800.
7. Glaziers 1694-1800.
8. Gunmakers 1656-1800.
9. Needlemakers 1664-1801; Pinmakers 1691-1723.
10. Basketmakers 1639-1824.
11. Distillers 1659-1811.
12. Makers of playing cards 1675-1760; Musicians 1765-1800; Saddlers 1657-1666; Tobacco-pipemakers 1800.
13. Pattenmakers 1673-1805.
14. Loriners 1722-31, 1759-1800.
15. Gold and Silver Wyre Drawers 1693-1837.
16. Tinplateworkers 1666-81 (gaps), 1683-1800.
17. Innholders 1642-43, 1654-1800.
18. Poulters 1691-1729, 1754-1800.
19. Upholders 1704-1772.
20. Paviors 1568-1800.
21. Founders 1643-1800.
22. Armourers and Brasiers c.1610-1800.
23. Coachmakers and Coach Harness Makers 1677-1800.
24. Ironmongers 1655-1800.
25. Dyers 1706-1746.
26. Cooks 1654-1800.
27. Masons 1663-1805.

## E. Professional groups

Brokers: registers of brokers, 1709-1869; lists of brokers' petitions (general, Jews, aliens), 1686-1786; brokers' bonds, 1697-1870. 24,200. *CLRO.*

Common lawyers practising in London, 13th-15th centuries. Large. *Ramsay.*

Lincoln's Inn men, biographical sketches of, 1600-1919 (covers those whose arms are emblazoned in chapel windows). 380. *Lincoln's.*

Police (Metropolitan) officers' records, 1829-onwards (from pension and personnel records). Incomplete. Large. *Metropolitan Police.*

Sites and monuments record, Greater London (contains some biographical data on architects, builders, designers). Large. *English Heritage.*

Survey of London: cumulative index to vols. 17-41 (builders, architects, landlords). Large. *Survey.*

Surveyors (mainly Middlesex), 19th-20th centuries. Small. *LMA.*

Architects, engineers, surveyors working for City, 17th-20th centuries. 1,100. *CLRO.*

For lawyers, see also Guy Holborn, 'Sources of biographical information on past lawyers', *The Law Librarian* **23** (1992), pp. 75-90, 119-135.

## F. Public Health

Bethnal Green midwife, diary of Millicent Francis, 1850-1, 1861-75. Names of mothers, dates of children's birth. 1,200. *Tower;* also M'fiche. *East of London FHS.*

Southwark St. George the Martyr. Petitions fc admission of poor people to Guy's Hospital (1776-80, 1783, 1786, 1795, 1797-8, 1800-1803, 1811, 1816) and to St. Thomas's Hospital (1803, 1809, 1820-21). Selon inde> *Shilham.*

## G. Foreign Residents

Some foreign communities in London ar much better covered than others in terms ( record publication. The Huguenot Society c London has been particularly active, as has th Jewish Historical Society of England (see fu lists in Mullins' *Texts and Calendars,* 195& 1983).

Italian merchants in London, 1350-1450. Large. *Bradley.*

Italians in London, 1841-71 (from census, 1841-1871, and St. Peter's baptismal records). Large. *Green (1).*

See also Professional groups.

## Cultural life, education, leisure

iarists (London, unpublished), 16th-20th centuries. 700. *Creaton.*

usical data in London newspapers, register of, 1660-1760. Covers musicians, composers, publishers, promoters. Large. *McGuinness.*

usic hall (London) database, 1865-90. 4,500. *Bratton.*

:alian opera subscribers in London, 1719-1750. 500. *Taylor.*

'anoramists, from 1780. 865 and in progress. *Hyde.*

heatre photograph collection, early 20th century. 200. *Westminster AC.*

3lackheath Proprietary School pupils and proprietors (covers Greenwich and Lewisham), 1830-1907. 5,000. *Rhind.*

ckenham, Middlesex, Church School. Records of pupils and teachers 1873-1929. *Hillingdon FHS.*

Rotherhithe: Amicable Society school minutes 1778-1870. *Shilham.*

Rotherhithe: United Society school minutes 1837-1873. *Shilham.*

Botanical Society of London, subscribing membership of the, 1836-56 (biographical data, scientific career, membership history). 371. *Allen.*

Royal Blackheath Golf Club members (covers Greenwich and Lewisham), 1766-1923. 1,000. *Rhind.*

Yorkshire Society's London school (Westminster Bridge Road), staff, pupils and benefactors of the 1813-1916. 1,200. *Creaton.*

Many published school and college alumni lists exist. See P.M. Jacobs' *Registers of the universities, colleges and schools of Great Britain and Ireland* (1964) and the Society of Genealogists' list of *School and college registers* (1988).

## I. Militia

See also Gibson and Dell, *Tudor and Stuart Muster Rolls*, FFHS (1989) and Gibson and Medlycott, *Militia Lists and Musters, 1757-1876*, FFHS (3rd edn., 1994).

Military and naval discharge certificates, late 18th - early 19th centuries (papers lodged with Chamberlain to register exemption from need to be Freeman of City to trade there). 4,000. *CLRO.*

City of Westminster militia ballot list, 1828. 30,000. *LMA.*

Volunteer militia lists: pay list, Bexley, 1803-9; Chislehurst and Footscray, 1803-5; Muster roll, Crayford, 1803. 500. *Bexley.*

Servicemen, 1914-18, mentioned in the *Bexleyheath Observer. Bexley.*

See also Monumental Inscriptions, page 18.

# INDEX

The following list includes all parishes in the City of London, the County of Middlesex and the Borou; of Southwark, with initials in parentheses indicating the ecclesiastical jurisdiction in which they fell probate and marriage licences, whether or not they have specific reference in this Guide. Parishes Essex, Kent and Surrey were in the main diocesan or archidiaconal jurisdictions unless indicate otherwise.

A = Peculiar Deanery of the Arches;
C = Commissary of London (London division);
DC = Peculiar Deanery of Croydon;
DS = Peculiar Deanery of Shoreham;
K = Peculiar of St. Katherine-by-the-Tower;
L = Archdeaconry of London;
M = Archdeaconry of Middlesex;
P = Peculiar of the Dean and Chapter of St. Paul's;
W = Peculiar of the Dean and Chapter of Westminster.

R = Consistory and Archdeaconry Courts of Rochester
(parishes south of the Thames from Deptford and Lewisham eastwards were still in th; diocese at the introduction of civil probate in 1858; see also Peculiar Deanery of Shoreham).
S = Archdeaconry Court of Surrey (diocese of Winchester)
(parishes south of the Thames from Southwark westwards were still in that diocese an archdeaconry at the introduction of civil probate in 1858).

This list, from Gibson's *Probate Jurisdictions*, FFHS (4th edn, 1994, updated 1997), is based, for th; city, on that in Lewis's *Topographical Dictionary* (1831), and includes places that may have bee; chapelries within other parishes and subsequently became parishes in their own right. Parishes were i; the city or its immediate vicinity unless otherwise stated.

St. Thomas the Apostle (L)
St. Thomas's Hospital 33
Tooting, Sy 18
Tottenham, Mdx (C) 18, 22, 25, 30
Totteridge, Herts/Mdx 18
Tower Hamlets 12, 25, 27, 29-30
Trinity in the Minories (L) 11, 18
Trinity the Less (L)
Twickenham Mdx (M) 29

Uxbridge, Mdx (M) 12, 18, 22, 26-7, 30

St. Vedast Foster Lane (A) 14

Walthamstow, Esx 12, 23
Walworth, Sy (DC) 31
Wandsworth, Sy 15, 18, 21, 23, 25, 31
Wapping St. John (C) 25
Wembley, Mdx 13, 18-9, 23
West Drayton, Mdx (P) 14, 18
West Ham, Esx 12, 18-9, 22-3, 25
West Wickham, Kent (R) 19, 22-3

Westminster 11, 17, 21, 23, 25-6, 28-30, 34
Abbey (W) 14, 17
Christ Church 18
St. Anne (Soho) (M) 25
St. James (Piccadilly) (M) 15, 21
Marlborough Street ward 19
St. John the Evangelist (W)
St. Margaret (M and W) 14, 17, 25-6, 32
Westminster Bridge Road, Yorkshire Society
London school 35
Westminster cemetery 18
Whetstone, Mdx 18
Whitechapel (C) 15, 18, 21, 25-6, 29-30
Whitfield's tabernacle 18
Wickham, East, Kent 19, 22
Wickham, West, Kent (R) 19, 22-3
Wigmore Street 32
Willesden, Mdx (P) 14-5, 18-9, 23, 28
Wimbledon, Sy (DC) 22
Wood Street Compter 25
Woolwich, Kent (R) 15, 22, 27, 31